REINVENTING TALENT MANAGEMENT

OTHER BOOKS BY EDWARD E. LAWLER III

Built to Change
Management Reset
Treat People Right
Talent

REINVENTING
TALENT
MANAGEMENT

PRINCIPLES AND PRACTICES
FOR THE NEW WORLD OF WORK

EDWARD E. LAWLER III

BK

Berrett–Koehler Publishers, Inc.
a BK Business book

Berrett-Koehler Publishers, Inc.
1333 Broadway, Suite 1000
Oakland, CA 94612-1921
Tel: (510) 817-2277   Fax: (510) 817-2278   www.bkconnection.com

Ordering Information
Quantity sales. Special discounts are available on quantity purchases by corporations, associations, and others. For details, contact the "Special Sales Department" at the Berrett-Koehler address above.
Individual sales. Berrett-Koehler publications are available through most bookstores. They can also be ordered directly from Berrett-Koehler: Tel: (800) 929-2929; Fax: (802) 864-7626; www.bkconnection.com
Orders for college textbook/course adoption use. Please contact Berrett-Koehler: Tel: (800) 929-2929; Fax: (802) 864-7626.
Orders by U.S. trade bookstores and wholesalers. Please contact Ingram Publisher Services, Tel: (800) 509-4887; Fax: (800) 838-1149;
E-mail: customer.service@ingrampublisherservices.com; or visit www.ingrampublisherservices.com/Ordering for details about electronic ordering.

Berrett-Koehler and the BK logo are registered trademarks of Berrett-Koehler Publishers, Inc.

Printed in the United States of America

Berrett-Koehler books are printed on long-lasting acid-free paper. When it is available, we choose paper that has been manufactured by environmentally responsible processes. These may include using trees grown in sustainable forests, incorporating recycled paper, minimizing chlorine in bleaching, or recycling the energy produced at the paper mill.

Library of Congress Cataloging-in-Publication Data

Names: Lawler, Edward E., III, author.
Title: Reinventing talent management : principles and practices for the new world of work / Edward E. Lawler III.
Description: First edition. | Oakland, CA : Berrett-Koehler Publishers, [2016]
Identifiers: LCCN 2016059388 | ISBN 9781523082506 (hardcover)
Subjects: LCSH: Personnel management. | Manpower planning. | Strategic planning.
Classification: LCC HF5549 .L28857 2016 | DDC 658.3—dc23
LC record available at https://lccn.loc.gov/2016059388

First Edition

21 20 19 18 17   10 9 8 7 6 5 4 3 2 1

Set in Minion Pro by Westchester Publishing Services.
Cover design by Kirk DouPonce, DogEared Design
Interior design by Jamie Tipton, Open Heart Designs

For Patty
My love
My reason for being

TABLE OF CONTENTS

PREFACE

The people who work for organizations are usually referred to as their employees or workers or maybe their human resources. Despite this, I prefer to use the word *talent* to refer to them. Why? Because I think it is a term that better captures who they are and how they should be managed. They are very valuable, often the most valuable assets of organizations. Because of what they can do, they determine how effective their organizations are. Increasingly, they are highly skilled and need to be managed in ways that utilize and develop their skills.

An organization's talent is not just employees who are expected to do a job. Talent comprises individuals who differ in what they can do and can learn, and what they want to do. To be effective, organizations need to manage talent in ways that makes it a major contributor to their success. Doing this requires talent management systems and practices that are not common practice or best practice in today's organizations.

Most organizations still use a job-based bureaucratic talent management approach that does not fit today's world of work and workers and will not fit tomorrow's. It is not enough to modify the old approach; a reinvention is needed. There is a considerable amount of research that shows what practices and programs will be effective in the new world of work and workers. It is thus possible to identify and specify the direction in which talent management practices should head and to describe in detail those that are being used by some organizations today.

This book identifies the major direction in which talent management needs to go and identifies specific programs and practices that will take it there. Consideration is given to the design and management of the key activities of an organization's talent management systems: attracting, selecting, developing, rewarding, and appraising. The book provides principles and practices that will reinvent talent management so that it will be aligned with an organization's strategy and become a key source of competitive advantage. It concludes with how organizations should be designed and led to effectively manage their talent management systems.

The audience for this book is anyone who is interested in the development and implementation of talent management strategies, principles, and practices that are effective in the new world of work, workers, and organizations. This includes executives and line managers in all functions who hire, develop, and supervise talent as well as human resource professionals in all types and sizes of organizations. Thought leaders at consulting firms and universities who are drivers of talent management principles and practices are an important audience, as are students of human resources, since they are the future of talent management.

THE CHANGING WORLD OF WORK, WORKERS, AND ORGANIZATIONS

Work, workers, and organizations are changing in significant ways, and at an ever increasing rate, and there is every reason to believe that both the degree and the rate of change will continue to increase. Most of these changes have significant and profound implications for how talent should be managed.

Simply stated, many of the old principles and practices concerning what makes for good talent management are obsolete as a result of the changing nature of work, workers, and organizations. What used to be good or best practice—or at least *good enough* practice—with respect to how people are recruited, selected, trained, developed, rewarded, and evaluated simply does not fit today's workforce and workplaces. These strategies, practices, and policies have become increasingly obsolete, and virtually every activity that organizations engage in with respect to how human capital is managed needs to be changed to become a best practice in this new world of work. This includes many of today's best reward, selection, and development practices.

So far the talent management principles and practices of most organizations have not changed significantly in response to this new world of work. They still follow a job-based bureaucratic model, focusing on job descriptions, equating fairness with sameness and seniority, and are managed by human resources (HR) functions that are not changing as fast as the world of work is. This has resulted in numerous books and articles that are critical of HR, some of which suggest "blowing it up."

There is considerable evidence that the HR functions in most organizations are not strategy driven and are not changing as fast as they need to. Table 1.1 presents data from my global survey of large corporations. The survey, which is done every three years, measures the views of senior HR executives on talent management and their organizations' practices. It is the only study that has measured change in HR practices on a global basis. The results show that between 1995 and 2016 there were no significant changes in how HR spent its time. In every country

Table 1.1 Percentage of current time spent on various HR roles in the United States

HR ROLES	MEANS							
	1995[1]	1998[2]	2001[3]	2004[4]	2007[5]	2010[6]	2013[7]	2016[8]
Maintaining records: collecting, tracking, and maintaining data on employees	15.4	16.1	14.9	13.2	15.8	13.6	15.2	13.2
Auditing/controlling: ensuring compliance with internal operations, regulations, and legal and union requirements	12.2	11.2	11.4	13.3	11.6	12.5	13.0	12.0
HR service providers: assisting with implementation and administration of HR practices	31.3[7]	35.0[5,7]	31.3[7]	32.0[7]	27.8[2]	30.4	25.7[1,2,3,4]	25.9[2]
Development of HR systems and practices: developing new HR systems and practices	18.6	19.2	19.3	18.1	19.2	16.7	19.0	20.9[6]
Strategic business partners: being a member of the management team; involvement with strategic HR planning, organizational design, and strategic change	22.0	20.3[6,7]	23.2	23.5	25.6	26.8[2]	27.1[2]	28.1[2]

Source: Edward E. Lawler III and John W. Boudreau, *Global Trends in Human Resource Management: A Twenty-Year Analysis* (Stanford, CA: Stanford University Press, 2015). Results from 2016 are new, and were not included in the 2015 book.

Note: [1,2,3,4,5,6.7,8] Significant differences between years ($p \leq .05$).

studied HR has spent and continues to spend most of its time on record keeping and providing administrative services.

The good news is that the major changes that have and will occur in the world of work are identifiable and will likely to continue to be. As a result, it is possible to make fairly definitive statements as to what the world of work will be like in the future. This in turn means that it is possible to specify what organizations should do with respect to talent management to be effective moving forward.

Talent management should become increasingly strategy driven, skills based, performance focused, agile, segmented, and evidence based. Before specifying in detail what talent management should look like, it is important to identify recent key changes in the world of work and why they demand new approaches to talent management.

GLOBAL AND COMPETITIVE ORGANIZATIONS

Organizations now increasingly operate in global business, social, and political environments because the products, services, and customers of most large corporations are multinational. Many industries are dominated by major competitors that are global in their operations; they produce products that are created on a global basis and targeted at global markets. This is true for the energy, automotive, and information technology industries, and for major services such as finance, consulting, and advertising.

Yes, there are still many businesses that are local, but they represent a decreasing percentage of the total business that is done in such places as China, the European Union, and the United States. Even those organizations that do not operate globally are significantly affected by the organizations that do; they compete for labor with them, and often find themselves doing business with and at times competing with global organizations.

One interesting example of the growth of globalization in the last twenty years is provided by food service and package delivery companies, both of which continue to "go global" at a rapid rate. McDonalds and Starbucks are prime examples of U.S. national food service organizations whose reach has become global in a relatively short period of time. FedEx and UPS have both gone global with their delivery operations. Information technology concerns such as Google and Microsoft have also gone global and in turn made it possible to connect organizations' worldwide operations.

One of the most important features of the global business environment is the ability it provides to internationally source the production and delivery of products and services. Information technology has made it possible to globally source talent for software development as well as phone sales and customer service. Many of the most obvious examples of this global sourcing are in the manufacturing sector: many products are partly or completely produced in countries that have low labor costs and, in some cases, easy access to natural resources that aid low-cost production. As a result, an increasing number of organizations now face global competitors rather than just local ones. This is true of both service organizations and manufacturing organizations.

A major factor that has led to the highly competitive, rapidly changing global business environment that exists today is the availability of financial capital. There is—particularly in developed countries—an increasing amount of venture capital available; as a result, individuals and organizations who wish to create new businesses or grow existing ones can access the financial backing they need relatively easily. There is no reason to believe that in the foreseeable future this supply of capital will decrease; the best prediction is that there will be an ever greater number of start-ups on a worldwide basis in decades to come and, as a result, the business environment will become increasingly competitive.

Strongly supporting the argument that more competitors will be created is the reality that more technology will be available to create new businesses. What happened in the case of information technology—with smartphones, personal computers, and tablets replacing typewriters, telephones, adding machines, and mainframe computers, and with social media creating new businesses—is likely to happen in other areas.

The globalization of business makes talent a global resource, and that raises many talent management issues. Organizations increasingly can and need to go where the "right" talent is available for the best price to be competitive. They need not only to source talent globally to be competitive but also to make good strategic decisions about how they manage talent coming from different national cultures. One clear implication of this is that an increasing number of organizations will need to manage talent effectively on a global basis, dealing with governments and other cultures—and the complexities they create—with respect to all talent management issues.

Perhaps the greatest impact the global business environment will have will be on the need for organizations to consistently improve their performance. What is good enough today will not be good enough tomorrow. This point was captured in the quality literature decades ago by the argument for continuous improvement, and it is even truer today. In fact, not just continuous improvement but dramatic improvement is often needed—not just in quality but in speed, cost, and innovation.

TECHNOLOGY IS A MAJOR DISRUPTOR

Technology—particularly in the form of information technology and intelligent computing—will increasingly be a major disruptive force when it comes to how, when, and where work is done and how it should be managed. Many previously repetitive, tedious tasks have been taken over by technology, and virtually all organization communication has changed dramatically as a result of such advancements. They will continue to have a major impact on when, where, and how work is done as well as what work is done. Already many individuals can and do work anywhere, at any time and, in many cases, with anyone.

There is also little doubt that we are just at the beginning of the information technology revolution. What people do, and when, where, and how they do it, is going to change dramatically and continuously over the next decades. How their performance is monitored and measured is also sure to change.

Organizations are increasingly going to need to be able to quickly change what they do and how, when, where, and how well they do it, as well as deciding who will be responsible for doing it. And they will need to change as technology makes certain products and services obsolete as well as the means of producing them. Just as no one sits at a typewriter today and prepares letters, in the future it is very unlikely that people will sit at a personal computer and send e-mails. It is inevitable that, increasingly, manufacturing tasks will be done by smart machines and by companies that globally distribute production based not just on labor costs but also on the quality and nature of the workforce, infrastructure, and technology in other countries.

Technology is driving and enabling the economy and organizations to use an increasing number of part-time and freelance crowdsourced workers who do work that has traditionally been done by full-time employees. The app economy is upon us, and it creates the opportunity for organizations to use various types of employment relationships that are flexible, adaptable, and can be driven by their changing needs for both skilled and unskilled workers.

Technology is impacting where and how work is done, and we are just at the beginning of this revolution. People will increasingly have the ability and all the tools needed to do many kinds of work and to connect with others around the clock and year round—virtually anywhere in the world. A key issue is how organizations develop a workforce, and how they coordinate and evaluate the performance of individuals who are not necessarily colocated but can communicate quickly and easily with each other.

Advances in computer hardware, algorithms, and data analytics will increase the work that machines do and migrate many kinds of work from individuals to technology-based operations. Intelligent computers are now capable of learning, playing complex games, responding to customers, and performing complex medical diagnoses and even some surgeries. This is an area where the rate of change is likely to accelerate as digital assistants are able to provide an increasing number of services in response to voice commands and IBM Watson–type computer systems are developed. In addition, the Internet is creating a world in which machines can connect and perform in ways that once required humans. Three-dimensional printing is changing manufacturing, and virtual reality is changing entertainment.

The challenge for organizations is to find the optimal balance between human- and machine-controlled operations and decision making. It is unclear how the new technologies will affect the total number of jobs that exist, but one clear outcome is that there will be fewer and fewer simple repetitive tasks, less human monitoring needed, and less supervision performed by managers. Another result will be that an increasing number of employees in complex organizations will be "knowledge workers" of one kind or another. Others will be talent that will be asked to work anywhere, at any time, on complex assignments that involve developing new technology and programming it. And more and more knowledge work will be done by computers as they develop more analytic and decision-making capabilities.

The best estimates tell us that organizations are just at the beginning of the disruption caused by changes in how, where, when, and with whom people work. Technology is moving rapidly in terms of the capability it has to solve problems, process data, learn, manufacture products, monitor activities, and connect people. Global organizations are likely to be leaders in the use of technology to increase their effectiveness in the areas of cost control, product design, production, marketing, sales, and internal operations. In order to do this they will need to be leaders in changing how they manage talent.

WORKFORCE DIVERSITY

In most organizations, many changes in the composition of the workforce have already taken place. These organizations' workforces are much more diverse than they were just ten years ago, and there are many reasons to believe that we will see continued growth in their diversity; this is particularly true in developed countries that have laws against discrimination based on age, race, sexual orientation, gender, or gender identity. The growing emphasis in technical and management education on the inclusion of minorities and women is another major contributor to workforce diversity. The age range of the workforce is going to go up, the gender balance is going to shift, and the workforce is going to include more transgender and ethnic minority people. Overall, most organizations will have increasingly diverse workforces with respect to every important characteristic of human beings.

Different age groups think about careers, and the features of organizations, in different ways. This seems to be a product of not only aging and maturation but also of the reality that people from different generations have different experiences at any given age. As a result, they look at work differently at any given point in time. Every new generation is likely to think, act, and look at work and careers differently when compared to how previous generations did when they were that age, because the world is in a constant process of change.

Organizations are just beginning to feel the full impact of age discrimination legislation and increases in life expectancy. These factors are leading more individuals to continue working into their seventies and eighties, and to a workforce that has more age diversity. This is likely to become even more common as health care delivery systems improve and people have longer life expectancies—particularly in less-developed countries as their health care systems improve. Another contributor to longer work careers is likely to be the need to earn enough money to "afford" retirement.

Organizations can no longer assume that they are dealing with a homogeneous group when it comes to the many features of individuals that are age related. They need to be able to manage and organize adults of virtually all ages.

Overall, organizations must be able to manage individuals that differ in age, gender, race, sexual orientation, and national origin. As a result, there will be very few organization and talent management issues for which there is an effective "one size fits all" approach.

SUSTAINABLE PERFORMANCE

The demand that organizations perform well has expanded over the last several decades in the sense that it is not enough for them to improve solely in terms of the quality of the products and services they produce and their financial performance. They are increasingly being asked to perform better in how they impact the environment, the society in which they operate, and their employees.

The social movement that demands that organizations perform better in the social and environmental areas has gained considerable momentum in the past decade and will continue to do so. It has resulted in new laws involving pollution and how employees are treated. Not surprisingly, it is putting the greatest amount of pressure on organizations in developed countries. They are under pressure to change the way they operate and to change the way their suppliers and subsidiaries in developing countries operate and do business when it comes to their impact on the environment and how they treat their talent.

As the world becomes more conscious of the importance of sustainable corporate performance, there is little doubt that corporations will increasingly be held accountable for their global impact on the environment, their employees, and the societies in which they operate. The demand that corporations meet what are often called triple-bottom-line standards and report on their performance is growing. As of yet this is certainly not being undertaken by a majority of the corporations in either the developed or the developing world, but there is significant movement in this direction.

Prime examples of organizations moving toward triple-bottom-line performance accountability are Google, Starbucks, and Unilever; they are ahead of the curve and showing some positive results. The more successful they are, the more pressure there will be on other corporations to follow their lead and perform well in all the areas of corporate sustainability.

ACCELERATING CHANGE

The changes discussed thus far in globalization, diversity, technology, and sustainability point to a very strong and important point: the rate of change is likely to continue to be rapid and increasingly disruptive with respect to traditional models of how organizations are designed and how they manage their talent. Most of our models of talent management and organization design assume a stance toward change that is episodic—that is, they argue for an analysis of the situation, an implementation of changes that are needed, and a period of stability until the next period of change needs to occur.

It is now well established that the traditional change model is no longer appropriate because it operates too slowly. What is needed instead is a continuous change approach in which organizations are agile and capable of constantly changing the ways in which they operate. They cannot rely on periods of stability during which they can perfect recent changes and plan for the next ones. Rather, they need to be constantly experimenting and changing what they do and how they operate in order to respond quickly to the rapidly changing environments they face. To do this they must have talent management practices that support experimentation, agility, and change.

TALENT IS CRITICAL

For decades, many chief executive officers (CEOs) and senior executives have said that talent is their organization's most important asset. In fact, this may not have been true for many of them, and it is clear that they have not acted according to this mind-set. Without question, for a few organizations talent always has been their most critical resource and they have treated it that way. But in the future talent will be the most important asset for virtually every organization. Simply stated, the changing nature of the work organizations do and the rapidly changing, highly competitive environment they face will make it impossible for most organizations to perform well without the right talent. As a result, talent will become the asset that makes the difference between winning and losing.

For most organizations, talent has always been a major expense. In developed countries, a common estimate is that 70 percent of the costs of a typical organization goes to pay and benefits. If you add to that the cost of recruiting and managing talent, the total cost of labor often exceeds 70 percent by a significant amount. Thus, it has always made sense to do a reasonable job of managing wages, benefits, staffing levels, and work performance.

But this situation has changed. Most of the changes mentioned so far in this chapter concerning work and organizations mean that decisions made about talent are increasingly becoming the difference-making determinants of organizational performance and not just key determinants of an organization's costs. Differences in talent performance effectiveness increasingly lead directly to differences in overall organizational performance. Because of this, superior talent management results in superior organizational performance. Those organizations that attract and retain the right kind of talent and treat it, reward it, develop it, and deploy it correctly, perform better than those that simply fill jobs with people.

Admittedly, in some organizations talent does not make a great difference with respect to organizational performance. Many bureaucratic organizations have been designed and structured so that individuals do not need to perform at a superior level; they simply need to perform at an adequate level. In many simple repetitive jobs in manufacturing, data entry, and maintenance, there is no opportunity for talent to perform at an exceptional level, and there is little advantage to an organization if someone performs at an exceptional level; an adequate level is sufficient. This is particularly true with respect to the work in an organization that does not make a great difference with respect to organizational performance.

The situation is different, however, when the performance of organizations depends on advanced technology, knowledge work, and high-value-added work. In this situation, which exists in technology, financial services, the entertainment industry, and many other fields, the best-performing talent is many times more valuable than the rest because it can make a significant difference in organizational performance. Similarly, in customer service situations, when individuals have to deal with knowledgeable and discerning customers the difference between good service and outstanding service can have a direct and significant impact on the bottom line of the organization. Thus, it makes sense for such an organization to focus on attracting, retaining, and developing individuals who perform at not just an acceptable level but an outstanding one.

The globalization and growing complexity of work are two additional changes that make talent an increasingly critical resource for an organization; they make organizations and work more complicated and require talent to have a broader understanding of management, organizational effectiveness, the global economic situation, and local cultures and norms to perform well. This means that getting the right talent may be more difficult, but it also means that it can provide a significant competitive advantage when that talent is obtained and managed effectively.

There is one additional point to be made about attracting and retaining the right talent in today's and tomorrow's work settings: such efforts have become more costly, and they will continue to be. It has always been true that training, turnover, and replacement costs depend on the complexity of jobs that are being filled. For some simple jobs, the cost is often only equal to a few weeks of pay; as a result, high levels of turnover are not a major cost for an organization. With complex work, the need for talented and well-trained individuals makes the cost of turnover much higher: it is often equal to six months or a year's salary.

It is particularly important that organizations that perform knowledge work and complex customer service work do an outstanding job of attracting, retaining, and developing the right talent. They can gain a competitive advantage by doing this simply because they have lower turnover costs, but that may be the least significant result when compared to the resulting performance improvements that come from having a motivated engaged knowledgeable workforce.

One direct effect of talent becoming a more important determinant of organizational effectiveness is that it brings more bargaining power: talented individuals can often "write their own tickets" when it comes to work deals. This has been true in sports and entertainment for decades, and has resulted in some amazing compensation and benefit deals; now it is increasingly becoming true for "superstar" executives and technical contributors. The amount of high-power talent most organizations need is going to increase as the complexity of their products, work, and services increases. Thus, the effectiveness of an increasing number of organizations is going to be determined by how effectively they attract, retain, develop, and manage their major talent.

Finally, the rate of change in the work environment and the agility required by organizations to deal with it increases the importance of maintaining talent agility. There is an increasingly high probability that yesterday's talent is not the right talent for tomorrow. As a result, organizations need to have agile talent management practices that allow them to continuously and frequently change the skill sets of their workforces. Talent agility is a difficult competency or capability to develop in organizations, and it increasingly makes effective talent management difficult. It requires organizations to take an agility point of view with respect to talent management issues such as pay, training and development, and job security, as well as the best use of part-time, contract, and temporary talent.

CONCLUSION

Recent major changes in work, the workforce, and organizations are shown in table 1.2. Each change is rated on its importance with respect to talent management and its potential for growth.

The globalization of work and organizations is rated as highly important. This reflects the tremendous impact globalization has on those who do work and how they should be managed. Moderate progression in this trend is projected in the next decade. There are some parts of the globe that have not yet come into the world economy and are not likely to in the near future. But many regions are producing more educated workers and performing types of work that were not previously performed in those regions. Thus, globalization is rated as moderate in growth since the political instabilities that are likely to slow it down in some parts of the world are not likely to occur across the entire global business world.

Technology is rated as a highly important factor in determining what work and organizations will look like in the future. This reflects the expected accelerated rate of major advances in information technology, robotics, sustainably effective ways to generate energy, and changes in transportation, as well as in manufacturing capabilities. Its high importance rating reflects technology's power to change the very nature of the work people do, where and how they do it, and how they are held accountable for doing it. It is rated as rapid in growth because of the many disruptive products that are likely to be created in areas ranging from communications to energy production.

Diversity is rated medium in importance; this is because although significant changes are required in how talent is managed, as diversity increases many of them are not as substantial as those required by technology and globalization. It is rated slow in future growth because the challenges that are involved in bringing new types of individuals (e.g., minorities, foreign nationals) into the workforce in many countries are and will continue to be significant.

The move to more sustainability in business models is rated as medium in importance for talent management and as moderate in future growth. It is an important factor in the careers and work choices of some individuals, but it is not an important universal issue. It is also likely to lead to changes in how some organizations operate, but it is not likely to quickly become a major objective for many. The reasons for this are clear: although in many developed countries there is increasing demand that organizations behave in a more sustainable manner, this is not yet a high priority global action issue (even though it should be). Many parts of the globe have not made a strong commitment to sustainability and, as a result, a rapid change by corporations with respect to how much attention they pay to it is not likely to happen.

Change is rated as highly important and as rapid in growth. These ratings reflect the cumulative effects of globalization, technology, and sustainability as major drivers of how organizations operate and perform. There is every reason to believe that this combination of forces will continue to increase in their impact and to create the demand for more agile and flexible organizations and talent management processes.

The final major change is the criticality of talent. This is of high importance because the many changes that are making talent more valuable and central to the effectiveness of organizations require major changes in how organizations are managed. It is rated moderate in growth because, though it may not grow at an extremely rapid rate, it is likely to become increasingly true as technology, diversity, and change require organizations to become more effective at talent utilization, talent development, and creating more agile talent management practices.

As can be seen in table 1.2, it is not a mystery where the world of work, workers, and organizations is going; it will be more diverse, competitive, complex, and challenging to manage. Workforces will be more diverse, technology will be increasingly disruptive, demands for sustainable performance will increase, and competitive demands will be greater. The convergence of these changes will create a new world of work that will not just call for it; it will demand new talent management principles and practices.

The challenge is to create organizations with talent management systems that are capable of responding to these changes. Talent management needs to be a priority in organizations because it can be a major

Table 1.2 Major changes: importance and growth

	Importance	Growth
Globalization	high	moderate
Technology	high	rapid
Diversity	medium	slow
Sustainability	medium	moderate
Change/Agility	high	rapid
Talent Critical	high	moderate

source of competitive advantage or, if managed poorly, a fatal flaw. This brings truth to CEOs' favorite adage: "People are our most important asset." Today's and tomorrow's challenges are to translate that philosophy into talent management and organization design approaches that recognize it and effectively act on it.

2

STRATEGIC TALENT MANAGEMENT

The dramatic changes that are taking place in the world are transforming work and organizations so significantly that traditional approaches to talent management are, at best, obsolescent. In many cases they are obsolete. They were designed for an era of stability, predictability, bureaucratic management, traditional financial accountability, little information technology, and slow change. Today we are in a world of rapid change, diversity, the high strategic importance of human capital, globalization, triple-bottom-line accountability, and radical advances in technology. In most corporations, all of these aspects are present today; and many of them are dominant themes.

Talent management needs to change in ways that respond to how organizations, work, and workers have changed and will continue to change. Doing this requires using the six talent management principles that will be reviewed in this chapter as a guide. They need to be the basis of all talent management practices and systems that an organization uses.

TALENT MANAGEMENT SHOULD BE STRATEGY DRIVEN

As is shown in figure 2.1, talent management needs to be driven by an organization's strategy and the capabilities it requires for it to be effectively implemented. Every strategy is only as good as an organization's ability to implement it, and its implementation is only as good as its

Figure 2.1

talent's ability to execute it. Because of this, organizations need to be sure that the capability demands of their strategy (e.g., agility, low-cost production, etc.) can be met with respect to how talent is managed. If they cannot be met, then the strategy needs to be changed. This relationship between strategy and talent is why figure 2.1 has a two-way arrow between "Strategy" and "Capabilities."

The five most important talent management practice areas are identified in figure 2.1. To some degree they are independent of each other, and they will be treated separately in the chapters that follow. Yet they are interdependent in many ways and need to fit with each other. Thus, they are connected by two-way arrows in the figure, and as we examine each one of them, we will consider issues of fit with other talent management areas. Only by using talent management practices that fit an organization's strategy and fit together to create an integrated talent management system can an organization be effective.

The reality that talent has become the key resource of many corporations mandates that it be a major determinant of most corporations' business strategies and that it be managed in ways that support strategy implementation. Much of the writing on talent management emphasizes that strategy should drive the talent management practices of corporations. Given the importance of talent, it is hard to argue against this point. To be successful, a strategy needs to be supported by the right talent management practices. But thinking of strategy as determining talent management is not the best way to state or think about the interaction of the two.

Yes, talent management needs to be influenced by an organization's strategy, but its strategy needs to be driven by the talent that is available to it and how it can be managed. A strategy that cannot be implemented or executed effectively because of talent availabilities and deficiencies is not a good strategy. It is just as likely to lead to poor organizational performance as one that is based on incorrect assumptions about financing, marketing, or production.

Perhaps the most obvious area in which talent should drive business strategy involves the availability of talent. The key to implementing every strategy is the ability of an organization to recruit and/or develop the talent it needs to implement and operate the strategy. Thus, there are a number of questions that every organization must ask when it develops its strategy: What is the right talent, and do we have it? If we do not have it, can we recruit and/or develop the talent we need to implement this strategy? Can we structure and design talent management practices that will lead to the type of talent we need to be motivated and willing to commit to the effectiveness of the organization? If the answer to either of the latter two questions is no, then the case is clear: the strategy will not be effective and should not be adopted.

There are numerous challenges to an organization's recruiting the talent it needs to implement a strategy. For instance, there simply may not be people in the labor market that have the right skill sets, or the organization may not have the assets it needs to make an attractive offer to the right talent. There are also many reasons why it can be difficult for an organization to develop the talent it needs; these include the willingness and ability of current employees to develop new skills and competencies, or the lack of the expertise needed to develop the skills of both existing employees and new ones.

In many ways, there is a great deal of similarity between the factors that are critical in recruiting new talent and those that are involved in obtaining financial capital when a new organization is formed. New organizations do not have a track record, and they need to sell the promise of future payoffs to talent. Not surprisingly, one of the major things that causes the demise of many start-up organizations is their inability to attract the kind of talent they need to be successful.

At the forefront of any discussion of talent availability should be a consideration of alternative approaches to accessing talent. For a host of reasons ranging from agility to cost and availability, the best way for an organization to get the talent it needs may not be by employing it on a full-time, permanent basis. Consideration needs to be given to the wide variety of talent access approaches that are available today and will be increasingly available in the future. These include contract employees, gig workers, employees borrowed from other organizations, workers hired through temporary agencies, and a host of other ways to temporarily obtain talent. Organizations increasingly need to think of themselves as being made up of constantly changing teams that assemble talent to meet the performance demands of a changing market.

It is increasingly common for organizations to take into account the availability of talent when it comes to implementing a strategy that has been decided upon. Talent availability is increasingly driving decisions about where organizations locate their operations. Further, an increasing number of organizations are using technology that allows talent to work anywhere, and at any time.

Most executives do recognize that implementing a strategy depends not only on having the right talent but also on being able to motivate and direct the talent to behave in ways that are strategically appropriate. But what it means to operate in strategically appropriate ways and how this can be accomplished is not always well thought out during the strategy development process; instead it is left for "later."

Leaving talent management considerations for later is a big risk, because it may not be possible to design an organization that has talent management practices that are conducive to the implementation of the business strategy. It is during the development process that organizations need to deal directly with how the organization can obtain and manage the right talent for a strategy to be implemented successfully. The next question should be, Does our organization have these practices and, if not, can we implement the right talent management practices?

Simply adopting a series of best practices with respect to rewards, performance management, recruiting, selection, and development is rarely the right answer to creating strategically appropriate talent management systems. Different strategies require different systems. Organizations must start with an understanding of what the talent management options are and an understanding of how the many options that exist impact the behavior of individuals and organizations.

Overall, developing strategic talent management practices is a critical and challenging task. To be done well, it requires an extensive knowledge of the alternative methods of talent management as well as an understanding of how they relate to the kind of organizational culture, competencies, and capabilities that are required to implement and operate a strategy. It also requires realizing that talent management practices may soon be outdated, especially with the way work and organizations are changing. Few "silver bullets" exist that can solve all talent management problems or can be strategically relevant for years or even decades.

TALENT MANAGEMENT SHOULD BE BASED ON SKILLS AND COMPETENCIES

Traditional organizations are built with a job-oriented, hierarchical mind-set. As a result, how employees are treated and managed depends more on the job they are doing than on their performance, skills, competencies, and needs. In the traditional hierarchical bureaucratic organizations of the past this may have been defensible, but it is not in today's world of work and will be even less so in the future. The management of talent needs to be designed to focus on the needs, skills, and competencies of individuals. This is the single most important thing that the talent management system of an organization can do to ensure that the organization will perform effectively and be prepared to deal with a dynamic environment. It means focusing on what skills individuals have and on what skills might be needed for an organization to be effective and evolve in an agile, strategically appropriate way.

In a job-based organization, how talent is treated is primarily determined by the hierarchical position it has. This includes how and how much employees are paid, how they are selected, the training they receive, their mobility, where they park their cars, where they work, what kind of furniture they have, and so on. In a skills- and competency-based talent management system, the key drivers—pay, recruiting and selection, training and development, where someone is located, and how someone is treated—shift. Such a system is focused on what skills an individual has vis-à-vis what skills the organization needs to be effective. Particular attention needs to be paid to determining and developing the skills that make a difference in organizational performance.

An organization will develop the performance capabilities that are aligned with its strategy, and the ability to change its capabilities when the strategy calls for it, only if a skills- and competencies-based focus exists. Thus, it is critical that the organization's talent management system and practices be based on skills and competencies.

TALENT MANAGEMENT SHOULD BE PERFORMANCE FOCUSED

The talent management systems in an organization need to be focused on the type of performance it requires from its talent to be strategically successful. The types of performance needed may vary from individual excellence to outstanding levels of group, unit, or organizational performance. Most bureaucratic talent management systems fail to take into account the complexity and importance of different types of organizational performance. They usually promise promotion and merit-based salary increases to the "best performers" and on the basis of seniority. This often is not the right approach, particularly with respect to promotions and to creating talent management systems that support organizational effectiveness. It ignores or fails to focus on the critical performance behaviors and talent development motivators that are needed to make the organization effective and that therefore should be the focus of talent management systems.

What is needed to develop talent management systems that are correctly performance and development focused is a strategic analysis of the type of performance an organization needs from individuals, groups, and the total organization to implement its strategy. This needs to be followed by a process that uses the results of such an analysis to motivate and develop the kinds of behaviors the organization needs at all levels and in all segments to be effective. These behaviors then need to become the key to what is rewarded, how talent is recruited, and how it is developed.

We can take as an example an organization in which cooperative and team behavior is very important. The right approach to rewards may be a group- or organization-wide incentive plan (e.g., a profit- or stock-option plan) rather than a traditional merit salary increase plan. It may also include training and development that focuses on cooperative team behavior. Finally, it might include a recruiting and selection system that is targeted at hiring talent that performs well in team-based organizations.

An important feature of every organization should be the attraction and retention of high-performing individuals with key skills. This ties directly to the reality that in today's work world the individual performance of key contributors plays an increasingly important role in the overall performance of many organizations. Because of the growing complexity of work and organizations, individuals can increasingly be the difference between an organization that is successful and one that just survives or, for that matter, fails. The reality is that more and more people are in critical positions in organizations because their individual performance has a major impact on the overall performance of their organization.

Increasingly, it is not enough to have someone who just gets the job done. For many types of work, organizations need people who get work done at higher levels than that being done by their competitors. This can only be accomplished by having talent management systems that focus selectively and strategically on the performance of individuals, teams, and the organization as a whole. Particular attention needs to be focused on work that is done at very different levels of effectiveness and has a key impact on organizational performance. Strategically important work that is performed at very different levels of effectiveness by individuals and groups is where the right talent management systems can have the largest positive impact on organizational performance.

Overall, talent management practices need to be aligned with each other and the organization's strategy and structure to create the mix of individuals and work units that can perform at a level that makes a difference. This can only be done if they focus on competencies, their impact on performance, and competitive advantage rather than on issues of fairness, seniority, and hierarchy.

TALENT MANAGEMENT SHOULD BE AGILE

The rate of change in what organizations need to do, how well they need to do it, and how fast they need to do it is continuing to increase. The only way to respond to this is to have an organization that is agile. The only way to create an agile organization is to have talent management practices that create talent agility.

What does talent agility require? It takes having talent management systems that are able to respond quickly and strategically to constantly changing labor markets and business strategy conditions. It is not a matter of having one or two agility practices; it requires a totality of management practices that allow organizations to adjust the kind and the amount of talent they have and the behavior of their talent on a continuous and rapidly changing basis.

There are a variety of types and degrees of performance change that organizations need to make in a rapidly changing environment. As a result, no single approach to creating an agile talent management system exists that is ideal for all organizations. Organizations may be able to develop a sufficient level of agility simply by constantly training and developing the employees they have. For decades this was adequate in the automotive and telecommunications sectors, but today it is unlikely to be sufficient because it cannot produce the rate of change and amount of change that is needed. It also may be very costly because of training costs and lost work time. To change more rapidly and at a lower cost, these sectors and others need to change their talent by hiring individuals who already have the skills they need or using talent that is not employee based.

The best approach for an organization to take depends on the nature of the business it is in, the labor market conditions it faces, and the rate and kind of change that is needed. What is clear is that an organization's talent management policies and practices need to be driven by the kind of change that it faces and by the specific needs that it has for talent and performance. Once those are established, it is a matter of putting in place the types of reward systems, career development programs, selection programs, employment arrangements, and other talent management policies and practices that will lead to the levels and kinds of agility that the organization needs to respond to its environment.

Historically, organizations including General Electric and IBM were admired for their career approaches to talent and for the kind of development programs they had for their talent. They provided *careers*, not jobs, and offered extensive development and training experiences. Many rewards were based on seniority and hierarchy, and employees might receive gold watches after twenty-five years of work for the company. Today's rapidly changing environment has made many of those approaches obsolete. As already noted, in most cases organizations simply cannot change rapidly enough by using training and development programs to change talent. Because of this, they cannot promise their employees a career, much less a job.

What an organization can promise is information about what its current business and talent needs are and updated timely information about how those needs are changing. Further, they can make themselves an attractive place to work for individuals who have the skills and capabilities needed at a given point in time. They also can adopt what Netflix does with respect to severance: the company promises its employees high pay while they work there, and a generous severance package if they are no longer needed; but what it cannot (and does not) do is promise everyone long-term job security. The reason for this is obvious: like many organizations, Netflix cannot predict with a high level of certainty where the business environment will go and what its future talent needs will be.

All that most organizations are able to do is control what happens today and put in place agile talent practices that will enable change. They know their staffing needs will change in ways they cannot predict.

Thus, instead of talking about job security, they need to promise to fully inform individuals about what they think the organization's future will hold and to treat people appropriately given the business situation.

Creating an agile talent management culture in an organization is not a matter of simply changing one part of its talent management system. Every part needs to be changed, starting with the attraction and selection process and continuing through the performance management process. The emphasis needs to be low on long-term commitments and high on communicating what the talent management situation is and what the organization will do to help individuals adjust to any changes that may occur.

The most difficult talent management agility issue is balancing retention and realistic promises about what the future holds. Putting great emphasis on promising a future for individuals whose skills may be outdated can lead to short-term retention but serious long-term problems for an organization, including wrongful discharge lawsuits and a culture of mistrust and deception. On the other hand, not retaining talent can lead to recruiting problems, extremely high levels of turnover, and all the costs and dysfunctions that are associated with turnover. Organizations must create talent management practices that do not overpromise with respect to the future and underdeliver with respect to the present. They must deliver a workplace experience and culture that attracts, retains, and motivates the kind of talented individuals that are needed to operate an agile organization. Talent management cannot be based on seniority and security.

TALENT MANAGEMENT SHOULD BE SEGMENTED AND INDIVIDUALIZED

The talent management processes and practices of most organizations adhere to a "standardization and equal treatment approach" that is oriented toward treating people who hold similar positions in the same way. Standardization is said to be the key to fairness, and fairness is said to be the key to good talent management. Sameness also leads to economies of scale. Treating everyone the same makes training, record keeping, and a host of other talent management practices less complex and less costly.

Certainly, sameness does represent one approach to fairness, but it is not the only approach or necessarily the best one. An alternative to sameness is to define fairness as treating individuals the way they need to be treated based on their needs, abilities, and performance and what is needed to make their organization effective. Based on what we know about the future of organizations, work, and workers it is clear that treating everyone the same is unlikely to be the best approach from either an organizational effectiveness point of view or an individual preference point of view. People differ, and organizations need to focus on how to take advantage of and accommodate these differences in light of their needs for performance.

The growing diversity of the workforce immediately makes the idea of similar or identical treatment being the best treatment for everyone null and void. What is good for a seventy-five-year-old is not likely to be as good for a twenty-five-year-old, even though they may be doing relatively similar work or working in the same function or unit. Similarly, what may be the best career model for an individual with a key organizational skill set may not be the best for an individual with a skill set that is not critical to an organization's source of competitive advantage. The same is true for an individual with a competency that is scarce and in demand versus one who has a competency that is easily available in the labor market.

Standardization needs to be replaced by a reasonable approach to segmentation and individualization when it comes to how talent is managed. The challenge is to create approaches to compensation, job security, development, selection, and other talent management practices that are legally defensible and fit the diversity of the workforce and the rapidly changing business environment that dominates today's world of work.

The operationalization of a segmentation approach can be facilitated by giving individuals greater choices so that they can create a work environment that fits their preferences. It also can be enabled through technology that makes possible administrative systems that allow individuals to make choices about when, where, how, and why they work.

The emphasis needs to be on reasonable individualization because without clear limits there is the danger that every employment deal in an organization will become a personal deal that is constantly changing.

This could result in a level of complexity so great that it overwhelms any administrative capability that an organization can create and manage—even while taking advantage of the power of modern information technology.

There is no simple, generally applicable solution to the challenges that are created by the need to treat different segments of the workforce differently. But it certainly is much more important and possible to do it efficiently and effectively today than it was before the web-based talent management systems that currently exist were available to help companies administer their human resources (HR) programs.

It is increasingly important that organizations develop and implement segmented, individualized management practices in all areas concerned with how they manage talent. There are few organizations that should promise the same treatment to all employees when it comes to key talent management issues. Of course, to some degree organizations never have; executives have always been treated differently from other employees; hourly and salaried employees have always been treated differently. The reasons for this range from legal requirements to the difficulty and cost of implementing different practices for multiple groups of employees.

The difference today is that organizations have a greater need to adapt and expand their approaches to treating people differently than they did in the past when they treated employees the same under an umbrella of fairness and efficiency. They need to communicate that the traditional job-level-based approach is no longer effective; it cannot be made to fit a workforce that varies as much as the individuals in today's workforce do—not to mention differences in when, where, and how they work. Companies need to replace the old approach with one that provides more choices and is aligned with the work to be done.

TALENT MANAGEMENT SHOULD BE EVIDENCE BASED

Given the importance of talent management practices and systems in organizations today and their greater importance tomorrow, they need to be based on evidence, not just common sense and experience. This is true in the case of decisions about how individual talent should be treated when it comes to hiring, pay increases, work assignments, and

promotions. It is also true with respect to which talent programs, policies, and practices are put in place in an organization. Given the increasing importance of effective talent behavior in organizations, it is time
to move beyond the practice of relying on what "seems right" and what
"makes sense" with respect to talent management. Decisions need to be
made based on research evidence and data.

There is an enormous amount of existing research that establishes
what makes for effective talent management. It ranges from research on
the effectiveness of secrecy with respect to pay, to how to select and
develop highly talented individuals. Unfortunately, too often this evidence is not taken into account when decisions are made in organizations.
Managers and executives assume that common sense and experience
are their best guides when they are making hiring and other talent management decisions. All too often they are wrong. For example, based on
their interviews of job candidates, many managers are confident that
they can pick the best candidate. But research shows that hiring
decisions based on unstructured interviews simply do not predict
performance.

There is no magic way to create more evidence-based talent management, but it is possible for organizations to move in that direction. One
approach is to do research. Today many organizations have a great
amount of internal data on performance and behavior as well as significant data analysis capability. It is thus possible for them to validate
their selection activities and other talent management decisions. Similarly, in many situations it is possible to measure performance to determine which talent, and which talent management practices, are best. In
addition, it is possible to gather data about the attitudes and behaviors
that predict turnover, absenteeism, and other critical aspects of the
workplace. Finally, it is also easier to calculate the cost of turnover and
other talent management outcomes that need to be taken into account
when decisions are made about talent management.

There is one additional factor that comes into play when organizations gather, analyze, and make talent policies and decisions based
on data from their workforce. It eliminates the "not invented here" reaction, which often leads to organizations ignoring evidence from studies done in other organizations in the belief that it does not apply to
them because they are different. Of course, they can still take talent

management actions that are not based on an analysis of their organization's data, but it is less likely in part because it will make them look bad. Google, IBM, and 3M have impressive HR analytic groups and have stated that having them increases the chance that their talent management decisions are evidence based and effective.

Of course, organizations do not have to do their own research to find out what talent management practices are effective. There are over 100,000 studies of talent management in the academic literature, and a number of very readable books that cover selection, training, compensation, and development. The bad news is that most of them focus on outdated best practices and must be read with caution when it comes to reinventing talent management; the good news is that there is a growing number that are relevant to how talent management should be reinvented.

Perhaps the best way of stating what needs to happen is that talent management needs to move from the category of gut feeling to the category of evidence- and data-based decision making. Organizations need to consistently and regularly ask and examine how their talent management programs and policies are working, what their costs are, and what outcomes are produced. They need to experiment with new approaches and determine if they work based on performance data. They need to use data to develop and manage individuals and their careers, and they need to provide data to individuals that will guide them in their career choices and decisions about skill development. In short, talent management needs to become much more data based and much more evidence driven.

There is a good chance that if organizations move to a more evidence-based approach to talent management, this will aid not only the organizations but also their talent. It is particularly likely to help organizations develop a more talented, productive, and cost-effective workforce because they will know the right way to treat talent and develop it. On the individual side, talent with additional data will be much more informed about how to develop skills, what career choices are best, how best to perform the work, and how long to stay in a job and with an organization.

In short, evidence can lead to better data-based decisions and practices that have the potential to create win-win situations. There is an increasing reason to believe it is imperative that individuals and organizations make more data-based decisions; they are a requirement in a world in which work is changing rapidly and both individuals and organizations constantly need to make key talent management decisions that affect individuals, organizations, and society.

CONCLUSION

The talent management principles and practices covered in this chapter are all focused on meeting the six work and workplace changes that were presented in chapter 1 and are intended to respond to one or more of these changes. Table 2.1 presents an analysis of how important and effective a response each of the six talent management principles is to the six major changes.

All of these talent management principles are important responses to multiple changes in the world of work. All of the workplace changes, with the exception of diversity, argue strongly for talent management to be strategy driven, skills based, and performance focused. The need for agility is strongly driven by the increased prevalence of technology; this change in the business environment makes it imperative that an organization build and adopt agile talent management practices. A second very important driver of the need for talent agility is change, which is often technology driven as well.

Table 2.1 Talent management principles and changes

TALENT MANAGEMENT PRINCIPLES	CHANGES						
	Globalization	Technology	Diversity	Sustainability	Change	Critical Talent	Average
Strategy driven	2	3	1	2	2	2	2
Skills based	2	3	1	2	3	3	2.3
Performance focused	3	2	2	2	2	3	2.3
Agile	2	3	1	1	3	2	2
Segmented	3	2	3	1	1	2	2
Evidence based	2	3	2	1	2	3	2.2

Copyright © Edward E. Lawler III and Center for Effective Organizations at USC.

Notes: 1 = little or no importance; 2 = moderate importance; 3 = very high importance.

Segmentation as a talent management practice is strongly driven by the two changes that lead to more diverse organizations: globalization and diversity. Technology and talent are also important reasons to focus on segmentation because they increase the need for talent to be dealt with in a targeted and individualized way.

Finally, an evidence-based approach to talent management is needed to deal with the importance of talent and the many complex issues that technology presents. Given the advances in technology and the resulting importance of talent, it is simply not prudent to allow decisions about the individuals who manage technology and drive strategy to be subject to decisions that are not based on the best evidence and data available.

As far as the changes are concerned, technology is pervasive in the way it affects organizations. As a result, having technology be anything other than a major driver of an organization's talent management principles runs the risk of creating organizations that lack the talent they need to develop and produce competitive products. The same reality is the reason that the importance of talent makes evidence-based, skills-based, and performance-focused management so important. The rate of change and the importance of talent also contribute to the high importance of having skills-based talent management systems.

Overall, the six talent management principles are useful and important guides in deciding which talent management practices will be effective in the new world of work. Thus, as we review how organizations should manage their talent, we will analyze whether particular talent programs and practices follow these talent management principles and focus on those that do because they are the practices that will create an effective strategic talent management system.

3

ATTRACTING TALENT

The increased importance of talent makes it crucial that organizations have the right talent. The staffing process begins with the recruiting process; it needs to be structured and operated in a way that attracts talent that is aligned with the organization's strategy and to do so in a way that prepares recruits to be effective employees. Accomplishing this requires integrated recruitment, selection, and onboarding processes that are targeted to attract, retain, and motivate individuals who can execute the business strategy.

The most important step in the process of building a talent management system that is able to attract and retain the right talent is the organizational branding. Based on their reputation, visibility, and the condition of the labor market, organizations need to create a brand and a recruiting process that attracts and retains the talent that will enable them to be effective.

THE STRATEGY-DRIVEN BRAND

The branding and recruiting process of an organization should be driven by and supportive of its business strategy. Therefore, developing an employer brand that attracts the right individuals should be an important consideration in an organization's business strategy. The business strategy will be a failure if it does not lead to the attraction of talent that can execute it. A key test of any business strategy should be whether it leads to and is supportive of an employer brand that will attract and retain the talent that is needed.

32

Instead of talent attraction being considered after the fact, it must be part of the strategy development discussion. Strategy creators should ask, can we recruit and retain the right talent given this business strategy? Obviously if it calls for bad working conditions, low wages, or performance and skill levels that cannot be achieved, it should not become the business strategy. If it calls for the organization to operate in ways that negatively impact the environment or society, it may not be able to attract the "right" talent, particularly if the right talent is young and well educated.

Organizations need to consider what the best employment relationship is in which the work can be done. It may be a full-time job, or it may be an independent contractor or gig relationship. Whatever it is, the employer brand needs to reflect that relationship to attract the right talent and give potential employees an accurate picture of what is expected of them and what working for the organization will be like.

All too often organizations make the mistake of assuming that to attract the right applicants they should do everything that they can to present to the labor market and job applicants a positive image of what it is like to work for them. This is an understandable but foolish strategy. There is a great deal of research that shows that organizations that recruit talent with an inaccurate employer brand tend to have dissatisfied employees and extremely high turnover rates; as a result, they end up incurring extra costs due to their high turnover rates, and they do not attract individuals who will perform successfully in the environment that exists in the organization because they block the self-selection process of individuals from operating effectively. As a result, individuals take jobs that do not fit their preferences and skills and organizations fail to attract those individuals that do fit. This leads to a strong recommendation: develop a realistic employer brand.

What does "realistic" mean? It means clearly pointing out what the pluses and minuses are of working for the organization and being sure that individuals are aware of what their work life will be like if they join. It is better to have people sign up for the "real deal" than to have them sign up for a false one. Having them sign up for a false deal will be much more costly in the long term and will create a situation that is more dysfunctional than losing potential job candidates because they do not like the deal that is offered. If there are not enough satisfactory applicants when the real deal is used, then an organization needs to look at why it cannot offer an attractive real deal, and that may mean it needs to re-think its strategy and how it operates.

KEY BRANDING POINTS

What should an organization's employer brand cover? Clearly it needs to say much more than "This is a great place to work." It needs to be clear that the organization's business needs are an important determinant of what work will be like. If the organization needs to be a technology leader, that needs to be made clear; if it needs to focus on customer service, that should be clear. It also needs to say how and how much it intends to take into account the trends that have been mentioned in chapters 1 and 2. It needs to address the type of leadership and management that individuals can expect, and it needs to focus on the goals of the organization and how that organization will relate to the society in which it operates. And yes, it also needs to deal with the rewards that employees can expect and what they will be responsible for. As will be discussed in chapter 6, it is critical that the rewards offered attract and motivate the talent that an organization needs.

Given the rate of change that exists, it is very important that the brand address the agility issue and what change means in terms of changes in the work to be done, employment stability, training and development, and long-term employment opportunities. To make things even more complicated, it may need to get into the issue of segmentation and differentiation and how this relates to fairness and equity. At the very least, it needs to make a commitment to individuals with respect to what they can count on in terms of continued employment and fair treatment. Overall, the key purpose of an employer brand should be to give individuals a realistic and comprehensive preview of what it is like to work for the organization.

Historically, many organizations have done a good job of developing an employer brand. Old favorites include AT&T, ExxonMobil, General Electric, IBM, 3M, and Sears, among many others. From the 1950s through the 1990s, via their ads, behavior, and presentations by their executives, these corporations gave people a good idea of what it was like to work for them. In many respects they had it easy in the sense that they had what was essentially a relatively simple and straightforward proposition with respect to what employees could expect in terms of job security, the work to be performed, long-term employment, fair treatment, leadership style, and corporate purpose.

It is much more difficult today for organizations to develop an accurate and easy-to-communicate employer brand. The complexities of the business environment they face and their value propositions require more complex messages. They need to send messages that suggest that working for them is not all positive, and they may have to send multiple messages because the need for segmentation and agility has led to them having multiple deals. They may have to say that how talent is treated in areas including job security and working conditions depends on what kind of work that talent does in the organization and include the message that they cannot make promises with respect to long-term employment and the future.

Currently there are a number of organizations that offer realistic strategy-driven employment deals that are very different from the traditional ones. Perhaps the best example is Netflix, which makes an extraordinary effort to present a realistic employment deal; its website extensively explains the advantages and disadvantages of working for the company. Some of the positives are above-market pay and an organization that has enormous opportunities for individuals to make money, use their skills, and do interesting work. The negatives are that employment stability is low to nonexistent and that unless talent performs at a high level, it will no longer be employed by the company but will get a "generous severance package."

Amazon is another company that has developed an effective—though for some, off-putting—employer brand. It promises a job with a growing organization, good pay, and opportunities for growth. It also stresses that it is a high-pressure environment and that individuals are expected to work hard and will have their performance closely monitored.

Many technology firms work extremely hard to develop unique employer brands. Google (now part of Alphabet) has done this very well. It receives constant attention in the press for the extras it offers its employees, including transportation, meals, gyms, and a 24/7 work environment. In return, Google expects individuals to be very committed and at times obsessed with working for the company. Not surprisingly, the

Google brand tends to attract younger talent and individuals who want their world to revolve around their work and information technology. This fits Google's business model and has produced a committed workforce.

It is difficult, if not impossible, to overstate the importance of organizations effectively communicating to potential talent their management approaches. Working in a traditional hierarchical bureaucratic organization is very different from working in an agile, high-involvement organization. Thus, it is important that organizations develop employer brands that reflect how they are managed and not just what they sell or how well they pay.

Other employer brands that are effective include those of the publishing company Berrett-Koehler, Patagonia, and Starbucks. They have recruited staff on the basis of being socially responsible organizations that treat their employees well and offer them extensive growth opportunities. For example, Starbucks has a program that supports its baristas getting a college education and pays salaries that are well above the minimum wage in most of the states in which it operates. It also focuses on recycling and the company's environmental impact. This represents a good fit with respect to the generation of individuals that Starbucks wants to attract, and it has produced a turnover rate lower than that of many of the company's competitors.

Patagonia and Berrett-Koehler have built their employer brands on the basis of their being benefit corporations. This form of incorporation allows organizations to behave in ways that are socially responsible and not focused only on financial performance. It is an enticing brand, one that gives the potential employer a competitive advantage in attracting individuals who are concerned about a company's social and environmental performance.

Once the "right" brand has been developed it is critical that organizations communicate that brand effectively to potential hires and monitor how effectively they are communicating it. They also need to have processes that deal with cases in which individuals make a bad job choice because either they do not understand what it will be like working for the organization or do not know how they will react to working for it even though they understand the brand. The online clothing merchant Zappos has dealt with this by offering new employees a bonus if after a few months of employment they do not feel they are a good fit and want to leave.

THE RIGHT BRAND

There is no employer brand that is the right one for every organization. Choosing the right brand needs to be driven by an organization's business strategy and the type of employees it needs to implement that strategy. It may be a business strategy that calls for a relatively homogeneous group of employees; in that case the right brand could be a relatively simple one used to attract everyone. Or it may be more complex because it requires a broad range of employees with respect to age, demographics, national location, type of employment relationship, and so on. An effective employer brand is realistic and supports the business strategy of the organization; it should be driven by the strategy and, once developed, it should change when the strategy changes.

The key skills that an organization needs should be a clear driver of the organization's employer brand and recruiting process. The brand needs to be developed so that it describes a work environment that will attract and retain individuals with the key skills that are needed to differentiate the organization's performance from that of its competitors. It may be based on social, managerial, or technical skills or a combination of them.

The skills that are needed may, for example, be more present among younger employees. When this is true, the brand needs to reflect the existence of the kind of work situations that attract younger employees. Many technology firms are good examples of building brands and recruiting processes that attract the type of talent that is key to making a performance difference in their industry. They have carefully built employer brands that are attractive to young information technology engineers.

The technology firms in Silicon Valley emphasize during the recruiting process the type of physical and social environments that are present in the organizations. They also talk about the flexibility, learning opportunities, and freedom that individuals have as well as the "life maintenance" support that employees get so they can live a lifestyle that involves high levels of commitment to their technical work. For example, these firms provide services that reduce employees' need to go to the dry cleaners, to cook, to wash their cars, or to perform a plethora of other standard duties that are part of being husbands, wives, homeowners, and parents but may distract them from their work. As an extra benefit, some organizations help pay off student loans.

Employer brands have always been segmented and should continue to be. The employer brand for executives has always been different from that of hourly employees. Yet this type of hierarchically driven differentiation of brands is not necessarily the best solution for the future. Yes, there should be segmentation, but it should be based on many of the factors that have already been discussed as key determinants of how talent management should be determined. The nature of the work, the culture and management style of the organization, and how talent management should operate in the future should determine the segmentation.

Segmentation should be partly based on the kind of skills and talent that an organization needs. Organizations need a brand that attracts the kind of technical and management skills that it needs. In the case of some organizations (e.g., those marketing consumer products and services), it may mean developing a brand that reflects a commitment to inclusion and supports diversity of many kinds. There may also need to be significant differences in an organization's brand that are based on geography and type of business. This is particularly likely for multinational firms and for organizations that are in more than one business.

The most challenging thing about building an effective employer brand is getting the right balance between a general brand and a brand that is specific to the employment relationship that exists for a particular job. The brand needs to reflect what the business strategy of the organization is, taking into account the geography in which it operates, what is expected of individual talent, and key local conditions.

To the extent possible, an organization's employer brand should be based on data that show what an organization's good performers see as the key positive and negative factors about working for it. This is a good place to start, because it is likely to lead to a realistic preview and attract high-performance talent that is similar to that already in the organization. The analysis of what good performers value and see as positive needs to be constantly updated to reflect the changing nature of the work and the organization. It also needs to reflect the specific situation an organization is recruiting talent for.

The result of a strategic segmentation analysis is often a corporate brand that is made up of a few key general points that are used on a corporation-wide basis. It is complemented by a number of segment targeted items that are used in recruiting particular types of talent to the organization.

It is worth once again stressing that whatever the brand is, it should be a realistic one. As noted earlier, bringing individuals to an organization based on an unrealistic picture of what their work life will be like is a sure path to failure: it can lead to high turnover rates, poor performance, and a negative corporate culture.

Finally, companies can and should monitor the attitudes and reactions of their new employees, job applicants, and potential job applicants through the systematic use of surveys. This will help to ensure that the interview and recruiting approaches used realistically portray what work will be like and that it is attractive to the right individuals. Such surveys do not need to use advanced information technology and big data, but those factors can make the process easier. There are firms that do surveys and publish the results (e.g., best places to work). Clearly such firms should be monitored, and organizations should also do their own surveys of the applicant pools that they are interested in to be sure that they have the type of attraction and recruiting process that they need to appeal to the right talent.

SOCIAL MEDIA

The growth of social media has created a new way for organizations to take their brand to the labor market and to determine how it is seen. Historically, employer brands have largely become visible to the world through print and broadcast media, advertising, business news stories, and interpersonal interaction with employees, customers, and others who have dealt with the organization. The growth of social media and the Internet has provided another source of information for individuals who want to find out about firms. It also can help organizations attract the right kind of applicants from articles on a company's website to postings by employees, customers, former employees, and job applicants on Facebook, Twitter, and other social media sites.

Organizations cannot control what is said about them on all of the platforms that exist. They can, however, control their websites and some, such as Netflix, do a great job of presenting what they offer and expect from employees on their websites. Increasingly, organizations are creating social media recruiting teams in their human resources departments that, among other things, have targeted interactions with potential job candidates and job applicants.

What organizations cannot manage directly is what goes on in the many chat rooms and social media outlets that allow employees to post reactions to the organization's actions, policies, and performance. What they can do in the case of these outlets, however, is monitor what is being said about them as a place to work. They can take this into account in determining how they recruit and hire, how they treat their employees, the kind of workplace they provide in the future, their internal and external communications, and how they deal with their employees and job candidates. They also can respond to what is being said on social media by posting corrections, information, and opinions that provide a realistic view of the organization. For comparison purposes, organizations should note what social media says about their competitors and analyze the posts to see how they differ from what is said about them.

A move organizations can make in the interest of positive attraction is to offer their existing employees financial incentives to identify and recruit strong job candidates. This can help influence employees to portray the organization in a positive light to their friends and on social media platforms. This, in turn, should increase the applicant pool and improve its quality. It is particularly likely to be successful if rewards are based on hiring success.

Just as organizations can control what is on their websites, they can also control what they post on many other sites, such as Glassdoor, LinkedIn, and Monster, which provide job searches and can help with recruiting. Organizations can also develop their own apps that provide job information about openings and answer questions. Given how much use is made of smartphones, this is a potentially powerful way to provide a realistic work preview.

ATTRACTING NONEMPLOYEE TALENT

One of the major changes in the business environment is the increasing use by organizations of nonemployee talent. As mentioned earlier, a multitude of employee relationships exist today between people doing the work of an organization and the organization itself. What has always been common in entertainment, construction, and seasonal employment situations has spread to many other types of work. Ongoing "not full-time" work arrangements vary from part-time and temporary employees to individuals who do work for an organization through arrangements managed by vendors, temporary agencies, and freelance talent websites such as TaskRabbit, Tongal, and Upwork.

Particularly worth noting are websites where individuals are listed and can be contracted on a short-term, project-by-project basis. Talent can be contracted for multiple short-term projects or one-off activities. Some "talent supplier" organizations run contests, and let the customer organization select winners to do project work in areas including advertising and software development.

A significant amount of the work of some organizations is increasingly being done by nonemployees who sign up for gigs in today's information technology–based economy. The work they do is not trivial; much of it is major work in advertising, software production, and financial analysis, and it is often work for which organizations want to attract the best talent available. For example, when an organization posts a position or project on Topcoder or Upwork, it wants to get the best talent available. To recruit the best applicants, it needs to develop a realistic and attractive employer brand and a deal for individuals who are competing to do the work the organization is offering.

Organizations need to develop a brand when it comes to how they treat contractors, freelancers, and crowdsourced talent because these groups often have multiple employment opportunities to choose from. Organizations that want to hire them should have a formal statement as to how such workers will be treated, and they should monitor social media networks to find out how they are talked about by individuals who have applied to work for them and those who have worked for them in the past. These organizations also need to work closely with vendor organizations and websites to be sure that they are getting good access to the best talent that is available.

Finally, it is important to do a careful and continuous analysis of the quality of talent that is available through different employment arrangements ranging from contractors to full-time talent. It may well be that the right kind of employees for certain kinds of work are not full-time ones; they may instead be available through Manpower, Upwork, or other staffing organizations, so attraction efforts should also be directed there. Whether this is the best approach is likely to vary tremendously from one type of work to another and from one organization to another; it can best be determined by an analysis of the quality of the work done by individuals from the various approaches and sources for accessing talent. The key is to determine where the best talent is and how it can be attracted. The answer may vary over time and is likely to depend on the skills sought.

CONCLUSION

The relevance of talent attraction to the changing nature of work, workers, and organizations is presented in table 3.1, which shows the talent management attraction practices that fit the six talent management principles outlined in chapter 2.

With respect to a strategy-driven approach, it is particularly important that the talent attraction process identify the key talent groups needed for the organization to be effective and that it be targeted at those groups. Potential employees need to receive a clear message about the strengths and weaknesses of the organization, with a particular focus on how and why its talent plays a critical role in its success and how employees will be treated if they join.

A strategy-driven approach relates closely to the second key principle, which is that talent management should focus on skills and competencies. The process needs to be based on attracting individuals with critical skills. Not all skills are necessarily recruited with equal rigor and focus; the recruiting message needs to be fine-tuned or segmented to target talent whose skills and knowledge are particularly important given the strategy.

With respect to talent management being performance based, the key issue is to make it clear that performance is rewarded and that it is particularly advantageous to be a high performer doing work that makes

Table 3.1 Attracting the right talent

Strategy driven	Target brand and recruiting process to attract key talent
Skills based	Fine-tune attraction based on key skills
Performance focused	Clear message about the importance of performance and how it is rewarded
Agile	Clear contract with respect to continued employment and need to change; use gig talent
Segmented	Multiple recruiting messages and approaches based on skills and strategy
Evidence based	Analyze who is attracted, why they are, and compare this to their performance and retention

a difference. Perhaps the best way to do this in recruiting is to empha-size that many rewards are tied to performance and to emphasize how much the best performers are recognized and valued by the organ-ization. It may be desirable to make the case that the organization is already populated with high performers since that can also be an impor-tant part of the attraction message.

Agility needs to be directly built into the attraction process; it is very important that the process emphasize the rate of change that will take place in the organization, and the amount and kind of job security and stability that will exist as a result. An organization that anticipates changing and adapting should make this clear in its talent recruiting and should explain what it will do to help if in fact it cannot continue to employ certain individuals. In short, this is a clear case where a strong realistic statement about job stability and long-term employment should be a critical part of the attraction process.

It is very important that the attraction and recruiting process be seg-mented. This is the only way that it can attract a diverse, skills-based workforce. Individuals with different skills typically need different at-traction messages and processes. These differences should be carefully built into the messages that are used, and the organization should be sensitive to the importance of skill and workforce diversity. It should also determine where messages appear and how they are distributed.

Finally, it is critical that an evidence-based approach be used to es-tablish, monitor, and change the attraction messages and processes that are used. This should include careful analysis of who is attracted as well

as the turnover rates for different types of employees. It is also important to study the reaction of employees once they join the organization
as regards to whether they feel they received a realistic preview of the work
situation and to analyze how effective different media are in attracting
the right talent.

It is clear that the attraction process can and should be guided by the
talent management principles that were emphasized in chapter 2. This
represents a significant change in how most organizations think about
attraction. It is very important that it be done to attract and retain the
kind of talent that is needed for organizations to be effective in the
future.

Developing the right employer brand and attracting the right talent
should not be left to chance; it should be undertaken carefully, and its
effectiveness needs to be monitored. Developing a brand should be a
very important focus because of its impact on the quality of the talent
an organization attracts and the relationships that an organization develops with its talent. A combination of increasing workforce diversity,
the need for organizational agility, and the increasing importance of
human capital make it ever more important that the right talent be recruited. The availability of social media, big data, and analytic approaches
makes it possible for organizations to understand what type of talent
brand they have and need, and what they must do to attract the right talent.

4

SELECTING TALENT

Talent selection decisions are an increasingly important determinant of success. For many organizations they are the most important decisions they make, often committing the organizations to high costs and major investments in time and analysis. It is not new that selection decisions are important. What is new is their growing importance as a result of human capital becoming a more critical determinant of organizational effectiveness. Also new is the technology that can be used to make them, and the need to shape the selection process to fit the new workplace and workforce.

EFFECTIVE SELECTION

The selection process needs to be carefully integrated with the attraction process. In many respects, selection is a continuation of the attraction process as it often plays a critical role in the decisions individuals make about whether or not to accept a job offer. The selection process says a great deal about what an organization stands for and how it operates; thus, it very much determines what kind of individuals will work for an organization and shapes its culture.

As an important part of the employer brand of an organization, the selection process must build on what is said about the potential employer in the attraction process and give individuals accurate information about what it will be like to work for the organization if they are selected. If it does not, the organization runs the risk that individuals will have false expectations and will become turnover candidates before the organization gets a significant return on the investment it has made in selecting, hiring, and training them. There is also the risk that it will be a negative experience that will drive away good talent.

In addition to being carefully integrated with the attraction process, the selection process needs to be an effective step in the onboarding process. It should introduce talent to the organization in ways that emphasize the organization's key features with respect to performance, learning, change, culture, management style, and interpersonal relationships.

The selection process needs to reflect the realities and challenges of staffing in today's environment. It needs to focus on the skills individuals have, make a valid assessment of what they can learn to do, and determine if they are a "good fit" for the organization's management approach and leadership style. In particular, it needs to focus on those skills that are critical for an organization's effectiveness. In many cases the process needs to go beyond assessing what is needed to do an existing set of tasks or a given job; it also needs to reflect what an individual can learn to do that is relevant to the business strategy of the organization and the rapid changes that are occurring in the world of work.

Given the complexity of most organizations, multiple selection processes may be needed. The most obvious basis for segmenting the selection process is whether or not the individuals being hired are development candidates. It may be that certain employees are being hired for an assignment that requires immediate performance, and the key issue is whether or not they can perform a set of existing tasks. On the other hand, they may be entering an area where a significant amount of learning is required and the expectation is that they will continue with the organization through multiple changes in work processes, technology, and organization design that require continual learning. As a result of this, employment candidates will need to be able to adapt to situations where development over a period of time is critical.

It is fair to say that a lot is expected of the selection processes that organizations use. It is also fair to say that many of them have not met those expectations. They have attracted the wrong individuals, they have resulted in wrong selection decisions, and they have given talent unrealistic expectations about what work life is like. While the selection practices of many organizations have continued to fare poorly, the importance of selection has increased.

There has been an enormous amount of research done on what makes for good selection decisions. It has produced some useful guidelines concerning what a good selection process should look like when dealing with the many complexities and challenges of hiring. There are multiple practices that are appropriate for producing good selection decisions and for helping talent make informed decisions about whether to join an organization. These guidelines can be used to develop selection processes that fit the new world of work and workers.

The major point that should be front and center when it comes to organizations making decisions about who to hire and what type of position to hire them for is that "past behavior is the best predictor of future behavior." This is particularly true when the environments and work are similar. Thus, it is very important to gather information about how applicants have behaved in the past and to base hiring decisions on that information. This is particularly important when individuals are being hired into positions where they are expected to begin performing well immediately after they are hired.

THE WORK RECORD

Since past behavior is the best predictor of future behavior, there is no better predictor of how an individual will perform in the future than how they have performed in the past. This means that when individuals are being hired, organizations should do everything they can to find out how the individual has performed in similar situations. Not surprisingly, the more similar the past situation is to the one where an individual will be working, the greater the predictive power of past performance data. Increasingly, data on individuals' past performance exists; in many professions it is widely available.

Sports is a very visible example of the great availability of performance data. Just about every statistic you can imagine is now available about the performance of athletes, starting from their junior high school years. Sophisticated and complicated measures are computed and used to make decisions about the effectiveness of football, basketball, and baseball players. In this respect, sports may be a bit of an anomaly with respect to measuring the effectiveness of employee performance, but it does not have to be many. Organizations already have extensive data about the effectiveness of salespeople, technical people, and the like. With the growth of big data and the increased monitoring of employee behavior through apps and wearable location and activity monitors, more and more information is available about individuals' performance. The challenge is to get good data and to use it in a way that produces good selection decisions.

Many organizations begin the data gathering process by asking job applicants to complete an application that focuses on their educational and work history. This is a good first step as long as the application is not so difficult to complete that it drives good applicants away. Increasingly, organizations are using apps as a way to make the application process more user-friendly. Such companies as Deutsche Bank, Ernst and Young, and Microsoft are using smartphone apps that help people fast-track the recruitment and selection process by playing games. This can encourage more applicants and send positive information about the organization and its culture, thus contributing to the attraction process. It can also provide organizations with behavioral data that can be scanned for relevant experience and skills.

Organizations often ask for references, and they can provide useful information, but there are always issues of credibility and truth when data are gathered in this way. Thus, it is very important that organizations do everything they can to determine the validity of data about the past performance of any individuals they hire. This may involve hiring vetting companies to look at the records of individuals and get data about their work and education history. There is also the option of asking individuals for their work records and accomplishments and then testing that against other sources; this is not only a good way of determining whether individuals are a good hire from a performance point of view but also a way to test their credibility and honesty. Frequently individuals do not provide valid information when filling out job applications.

INTERNSHIPS, GIGS, AND SIMULATIONS

Without question, the best way to give individuals information about what it is like to work in an organization and to give that organization information about whether an individual can do the job is to have them actually work at the job or a simulation of it. This is always better than doing interviews or using tests that give information about people's personalities, skills, and abilities but may not predict job performance. Having job candidates actually do the job tells an organization if individuals can accomplish specific tasks; it can also make it clear to those individuals what it is like to do the work the organization wants them to.

One interesting process that can be used to test individuals is the blind audition. In symphony orchestras, this involves auditioning for jobs behind a screen so that the hiring managers are forced to pay attention to what matters most: how well those auditioning play their instruments; the managers are not distracted or influenced by appearance, race, gender, and the like. These blind audition practices fit well as an initial screening process for collecting work samples from writers, coders, customer service representatives, researchers, and others who are being considered to do technical and administrative work.

There are multiple ways to have individuals do the work that the organization has to offer without hiring them on a regular employment basis. The most obvious is the use of temporary work programs, such as internships, contract hires, and temporary assignments. Internships have long been used as an effective selection device. Many companies use them as a way to attract, test, and ultimately select college and high school students as well as others who are interested in developing themselves. They combine a realistic job preview with a work sample, and thus can improve both the attraction and selection processes of an organization. They are an effective way to select and manage talent in the new world of work and workers.

Temporary work assignments and internships can last a matter of hours or many months—even years. In many respects, the longer the time period, the better. This gives the organization time to observe individuals actually doing the work that they would be doing as employees and gives individuals a chance to see what the organization and the work is like. Admittedly, it is one thing to be a regular employee and another to be a temporary employee or intern. Even so, the temporary work assignment is a much better way to give potential employees a sense of what the organization and the work is like versus having them observe it or having somebody explain it to them. And, needless to say, it is also the best way to test whether they can do the work.

The information technology revolution provides many new opportunities to have individuals do work for organizations before they become regular employees. Gig sites provide the opportunity for organizations to get work samples that can be very valuable in determining what an individual can do and whether the organization wants to employ somebody for a gig or on a regular basis. Technology also provides the opportunity to simulate work situations in ways that have not been possible before. Simulations can be interactive and can test the responses of applicants to evolving situations and technical problems; they can make testing much more realistic and therefore more valid. Video games may also be a good choice, as they have the potential to create simulations that test the judgment and analytic capabilities of potential hires. They have the advantage of putting individuals in work situations and being able to see how they analyze and respond to them.

Overall, the best way to judge if potential employees can do something is to have them do it, not to ask them or others (past employers, coworkers, etc.) whether they can do it. Of course, it may not always be possible to observe somebody performing work, so it may be necessary to get data about their performance history. This can be extremely valuable when the source of the data is credible and the work that the applicant has done previously is similar. If the job entails producing a manuscript, film, advertisement, or other identifiable product, a good substitute is an assessment of the work product itself. Unfortunately, job candidates themselves are frequently not a valid source of performance data and it is often impossible to find someone who is.

ABILITY AND PERSONALITY TESTING

For a variety of reasons, organizations cannot always obtain a work sample: applicants may require specific training for the work to be done, or the work may simply be too complex or involve too long a time span to do for those who are not actual employees. It may not even exist in "doable" form because the first work of applicants is to develop the project or work that they will be doing. In these cases, an intelligence or targeted ability test may be the best choice.

Standardized psychological tests can be useful when they measure an ability like intelligence, which is critical to most or all work that might be performed by job applicants. Skill and ability tests are particularly useful when the work entails learning to perform tasks that applicants may not have any prior experience with.

Organizations have used many different personality and interest tests for decades. The most popular and most frequently used of these is the Myers-Briggs Type Indicator; among other questions, it asks a job applicant to say whether he or she would rather be considered a "practical person" or an "ingenious person" and whether he or she is a "good talker" or instead "quiet and reserved." One estimate is that over fifty million people around the world have taken the test.

The research evidence shows that, in most cases, personality tests are not valid predictors of job performance. There is reason to believe that they can be predictive for some kinds of work (e.g., customer contact roles), but that as a general rule they are not good predictors of performance and thus should not be used for selection unless they have been shown to be valid by studies that are specific to the work that will be done by the talent being tested.

INTERVIEWS

The most frequently used selection tool is the one-on-one interview. Most interviews are unstructured (the interviewer asks whatever he or she wants) and often turn out to be rambling conversations between the interviewer and the job candidate. Not surprisingly, most interviews have little or no validity when it comes to predicting the performance of job candidates or the length of their employment. Despite this, the interview continues to be the most frequently used selection device.

Many managers feel that they can make good selection decisions about job candidates based on their ability to do interviews. Research on selection decisions does not support this conclusion; it does show that most managers believe they can make good decisions, but it does not support the notion that they actually do so. Interviews are also flawed with respect to giving job candidates an accurate view of what work will be like once they join an organization.

The validity record of interviews suggests that it may be best to never have interviews as part of the selection process in the new world of work and workers. The problem with this is that most applicants want to have interviews so that they can meet the individuals they will potentially be working with and for, and managers also want to know and have a say in who is hired. Having them approve a new hire after an interview also helps commit them to a successful onboarding of that hire. Thus, rather than eliminating interviews, the best solution is often to direct interviewers toward the realistic preview and attraction side of what an effective selection process needs to accomplish and have them play little or no role in actual hiring decisions.

As far as contributing to valid selection decisions and attraction, it is critical that interviews be structured and guided by a predetermined list of key questions and points. There is a large amount of evidence that shows that when there is little structure to interviews, interviewers tend to ask questions that are inappropriate, invalid, and in some cases discriminatory, unethical, and even in violation of labor laws. For example, they sometimes ask about childhood experiences, what job applicants' parents are like, what their hobbies are, and a whole list of things that are not valid predictors of the future performance of the prospective employees.

Adam Bryant interviews chief executive officers and publishes the results every Sunday in the *New York Times*. He always asks, "How do you hire?" The CEOs all report on what they ask in interviews and almost without exception they ask about something that is not likely to be a predictor of performance. For example, "If you had all the money in the world, and you had one year to live, what would you be doing?" or "What do you do on weekends?"

Questions should be directly targeted at evaluating how well individuals have previously performed work that is similar to the work that they are applying to do. The same structured questions should be asked of all interviewees so that comparisons can be made. The questions need to focus on the kind of skills needed for someone to do or learn how to do the work they are being hired to do. There is evidence that this type of interview can be valid in selecting some employees. When structured interviews are done, there is also much less chance that the interviewer will ask questions that are inappropriate, invalid, or inaccurately communicate what it is like to work for the organization.

It often makes sense to have structured interviews that are guided by information technology. To assure that the right questions are asked across multiple interviews, a key list of questions can be developed and sent to all interviewers. As the interview process unfolds, the interviewers can connect with each other about what has been answered, which issues to pursue, and which question should be focused on. This is a good way to improve the practice of interviewing and to ensure that interviews are valid, ask reasonable questions, and are not repetitive.

Interviews should be structured in a way that informs job candidates about what will be expected of them and what it will be like to work in the organization. Giving the job candidate a good preview of what work will be like is a much more achievable goal than having the interviewer make a valid hiring decision based on information that is provided by the job applicant in response to interviewer-created questions.

Making an interview effective requires training the interviewer to deliver the right kind of information and to ask appropriate questions. It is not an easy task, but it is one that can be accomplished and will lead to much better results than unstructured, rambling interviews that focus on what an untrained interviewer thinks will predict whether or not the interviewee will be a good employee.

The point made earlier about past behavior being the best predictor of future behavior suggests that structured interviews should focus on asking individuals what they have done and how they behaved in previous job situations. Interviews should be constructed to carefully look at the responsibilities individuals had in previous jobs and to get them to talk about particular incidents in the workplace that they encountered and how they responded to them. Job applicants should also be asked what kind of tasks they performed, what knowledge was required to perform them, and how they dealt with new challenges and learning opportunities. It may also be effective to ask what they learned from their past work and how they will approach work in the future.

It is worth repeating that the interviews should be considered part of the attraction process. Clearly, job applicants develop feelings of like or dislike for interviewers during the interview process. This can make a big difference in whether they end up completing the selection process and accepting a job if it is offered. It is thus important that the interviewer conduct the interview in a way that produces a positive dialogue with the job applicant.

Finally, there is the possibility of having interviews that have no influence on selection decisions. I have seen this approach work well in situations where there is a clear record of candidate performance available; it is assessed, the hiring decision is made, and then the individual is invited to an interview. Done well, these interviews can provide a chance for the interviewers and interviewees to exchange information about the culture and climate of the organization and to start the onboarding process of those individuals who will ultimately be hired.

SOCIAL MEDIA

The increasing use of social media can provide organizations with new means to find out about an individual's past behavior. They can simply go to prospective employees' Facebook accounts or other postings and see what kind of interests they have, how they behave, how they respond to friendships and networks, and so on. The challenge with information gleaned from social media is determining its relevance to the work to be performed.

In many cases, social media information may be irrelevant because the issues in it are very different from those of the work situation. There may, however, be instances in which individuals on social media forums state things or behave in ways that are simply unacceptable and do not represent what a company would like its employees to be known for. Looking at behaviors that are extreme also can provide meaningful warnings about how individuals might represent the company and how they might behave in the workplace.

Perhaps the best way to think about the relevance of social media is that it is a new and potentially useful source of information. Social media forums should be treated as just one source of information about how an individual behaves, but they are a valid source of information about behavior. What candidates post on social media is an example of how they represent themselves and therefore a possible indicator of how they will behave in the workplace.

VALIDATION

Validation is a must for all selection processes. For a number of reasons, it is very important that organizations determine whether the methods and processes they are using to select employees produce valid decisions. The results of the selection process need to be tested on a continuing basis against turnover, absenteeism, productivity levels, and other performance measures. Given the rate of change in the world of work, old results are not good enough. A few years ago, continuous validation may not have been necessary; today, as work and workers change at an accelerating rate and new sources of data multiply (e.g., social media, gaming, etc.), validation should not be looked at as a one-off but as a continuing process. Validation should look at all the elements in the selection process that influence final decisions. It should also always involve looking for new practices that will improve the selection process.

In jobs where there is a high variance in performance, a small increase in the validity of the selection process can result in an enormous gain in the performance of individuals and ultimately in the performance of organizations. In the cases where the top performers are ten to twenty times more productive than average performers (which is often true for technical work such as software engineering), even a small increase in predictive validity can result in a big performance gain. In such work situations, having a valid selection process is particularly important.

Validation is important not just because it can lead to improved selection decisions, and better cost and productivity numbers in an organization; it also provides a defense against lawsuits, charges of discrimination, and unfair employment actions. This is where information technology and the era of big data come into play. It is much easier today to get performance data about individuals, and to use data analytics to determine how predictive the various parts of a selection process are.

DECISION MAKING

In traditional organizations, job applicants are interviewed and selected in a highly hierarchical process; they are interviewed by managers and the hiring decision is made by their boss-to-be and maybe his or her boss. Future peers, subordinates, and other employees have little or no participation in the interview and selection process. This traditional hierarchical management approach does not fit the new world of work and workers because it fails to build a commitment to the outcome of the process and ignores helpful information that future peers and subordinates may have about whether a job candidate should be hired.

Many technology firms and some retail firms (e.g., Whole Foods) recognize the importance of including future coworkers from all organization levels in the selection process. They have future peers and subordinates interview job candidates and in some cases vote on the selection decision. This has the obvious advantage of building their commitment to the success of the new hire and may provide valuable selection information. It also brings the selection process more in line with the world of work as it exists in high-performance organizations. That said, a word of caution is in order here with respect to who votes on the hiring. As already noted, interviews often are not valid selection methods. Thus, it often is best to give peers and subordinates only veto power with respect to preselected top candidates.

SEGMENTATION

It is obvious that the same selection processes and practices cannot be used throughout large, complex organizations; there are simply too many differences in the skills needed, the kind of working conditions individuals face, and the messages that need to be delivered to talent. Multiple selection practices need to be developed that fit the skills that are needed in particular parts of an organization. These practices also need to fit the nature of the work that is to be done. What should be common across the selection processes that are used in different parts of an organization is that they attract the right individuals, provide a realistic preview, and have been found to be valid predictors of performance.

Given the reality that how some work is done is a particularly important determinant of organizational performance, the selection decisions for certain jobs need to get special attention. In traditional organizations, higher-level jobs have always gotten special attention. The difference in the new world of work is that hierarchy should not be the major determinant of which jobs get such attention; it should be given to selecting individuals to do the work that is critical to organizational performance and is subject to wide performance variation. This might be work in research and development or in customer service. In the case of Disney, one critical job is maintenance and cleaning in the company's theme parks, because individuals in these jobs have important interactions with customers when they are asked for directions and help. In the case of real estate, sales agents are critical; the best produce many times more sales than other agents.

CONCLUSION

Selecting the right talent for an organization is an increasingly challenging and important activity. Because organizations have become more talent dependent, there is less and less room for making bad selection decisions and for using selection practices and processes that do not attract the right talent. Many traditional best practices are obsolete because of the changes that have occurred in the world of work and workers.

As can be seen in table 4.1, it is particularly important that strategy drive a focus on the selection of employees for key work. This means that a disproportionate percentage of selection time and effort should be spent on a relatively small percentage of jobs. Of course, careful selection is needed for all the work in the organization, but some work warrants considerably more attention.

The selection approaches that organizations use need to vary based on the nature of the skills that are needed to do the work well. As table 4.1 shows, it is very important to assess the skills that individuals have by looking carefully at test results and using work simulations, structured interviews, and work histories. This point once again emphasizes the reality that the best predictor of future behavior is past behavior. This leads to the point that selection should be based on past performance; this is particularly true when the work to be done is similar and there is a chance to observe and validate how a person has performed in the past. This can be done when organizations use

Table 4.1 Selecting the right talent

Strategy driven	Focus on selection for key work and behaviors
Skills based	Use tests, work history, simulations, and structured interviews
Performance focused	Assess past performance; use internship and work samples
Agile	Look at history of skills and skills development
Segmented	Use work-specific selection practices; focus on work that makes a difference
Evidence based	Validate all selection practices and decisions on a continuous basis

internships, take work samples, and use simulations and work-related tests.

To be sure that an organization develops an agile workforce, talent selection may require some targeted practices. One is to hire short-term gig or contract employees. The other is to look at the history of individuals and determine whether they have been flexible and agile in their work lives. Have they, for example, changed jobs frequently, learned new skills, and gone to training programs? An agility analysis is particularly important if an organization is committed to developing employees either because the skill sets they need simply are not available in the general population or because an organization is experiencing rapid changes in its business environment, technology, and/or product mixes that are best responded to by long-term employees.

With respect to segmentation, much of the selection process needs to be targeted at the specific skill set needed to do the work for which the individual is being hired. This means that selection methods and practices may differ significantly for different parts of the organization and for different hiring situations; they need to be designed for the work individuals are expected to do and the part of the organization they will be in.

Finally, table 4.1 shows that it is important to validate the selection practices and decisions of organizations on a continuous basis. This is increasingly possible with the big data and analytics capability that is now available, and increasingly important because of the changing nature of work and the work environment. What may be a good predictor of performance at one point in time may quickly become a poor predictor later because the work and/or the environment in which it is performed has changed. Perhaps the best way to summarize is to say that the selection process needs to become data driven, and the data should be collected and analyzed on a continuous basis.

5

DEVELOPING TALENT

Developing the right talent and doing so in the right way is critical to the effectiveness of every organization. For a long time the iconic talent development and management organizations were the career-oriented ones; human resources (HR) articles and books were full of reports on the programs run by AT&T, General Electric, IBM, Procter & Gamble, and other corporations that had well-developed career development models. These organizations did an outstanding job of identifying the talent that needed to be developed, specifying what skills needed to be learned, and providing the kind of learning experiences that would develop the skills they needed. They provided the benchmarks against which many companies evaluated their talent development programs.

To say that things have changed with respect to what should be done in the area of talent development is an understatement. No longer are the talent models that were considered benchmarks looked to as best practices. Today they are seen as outdated and, in most cases, inappropriate given today's work and workers. The major reason for this is the many changes that have occurred in the workforce, as well as the development of new technology and the need for organizations to be agile. Simply stated, long-term company-wide career development programs like those that dominated the best practice literature in the last half century simply do not fit today; they fail to provide the talent motivation and agility that organizations need. This, of course raises a key question: What is the right approach today, and what is likely to be the best practice in the future?

STRATEGY-DRIVEN TALENT

The best starting point for thinking about the best talent development practices is to examine the organization's business strategy and the rate of change it expects to experience. It should determine what kind of talent development activities an organization engages in, who should be developed, and what kind of development candidates will receive. The focus needs to be on the identification of the skills an organization needs to be effective and how it should position itself with respect to obtaining those skills.

The strategic analysis should begin by identifying what the key levels and kinds of performance are for the organization and how long they are likely to be needed; it should then, based on this analysis, identify what key skills the organization needs. The analysis should focus on determining the business skills, technical skills, and customer service skills that are key to the execution of the business strategy. Clearly these skills should get the highest priority with respect to development.

Once an analysis has been done that determines the needed skills, it is important to look at the pool of individuals with those skills. It is likely that some of the skills can be easily obtained in the labor market while others cannot, either because they are idiosyncratic to the organization or because market demand for them is strong.

After an organization has completed an analysis that looks at the skills it needs and the degree to which they are available in the labor market, it can then proceed to working on a plan for developing and obtaining the talent it needs. This is easier to say than it is to execute, but the key here is that an organization should commit to developing only skilled talent that cannot be easily obtained in the labor market. Further, the focus should be on skills that are critical to the overall success of the organization and implementation of its strategy.

THE TALENT MIX

A key strategic issue for any organization is what mix of talent development and employment models it should have. What kind and how many, if any, employees should be treated as development candidates and core employees of the organization, and what kind and how many should be treated as "traditional" employees? How many and what kind should be part-time, temporary contractors, or gig workers? The answers to these questions depend on what kind of business strategy the organization has and the environment that it faces. Making the right choices is critical to an organization's ability to be effective in the long term. Wrongly investing in talent is a sure route to unsustainable costs and economic problems, as is not investing in developing skilled talent that is not readily available in the labor market. Having the right kind and amount of talent is the road to organizational effectiveness.

The key issue for an organization is identifying and positioning itself where it should be in terms of the number and type of employees that it has in its different talent development, retention, and employment models. It must decide which kind of skills and competencies fall in the active company development area and which can be obtained in the labor market. This is where supply and demand in the labor market becomes critical and the issue of the core competencies of the organization comes into play. A general rule is that if talent can be obtained in the labor market, it should be.

Correctly positioning an organization with respect to its talent mix strategy increasingly requires it to have multiple talent models. Talent segmentation is required to reflect the realities of the labor market, the changing nature of skills the organization needs, and the agility demands that the organization faces. This is not a new situation; most organizations have operated with several different types of talent development models for decades. Organizations typically have approaches for their salaried employees that differ from what they have for their hourly ones. What is new is the reasons for having segmentation and the types and extent of segmentation that are needed.

In the future, segmentation needs to be practiced by most organizations and be based not on hierarchy but on an organization's strategy, the labor market, and its needs for agility. This will mean that hierarchy and tradition will be much less important in determining the types of employment deals an organization offers, and it most certainly will lead to it offering multiple deals. The segmentation may be like that in the motion picture business and construction industries, which have always had multiple, very different, development models for their talent. They invest in some employees (e.g., producers or senior managers, respectively), while others (e.g., actors or building contractors) are "on their own," and in some cases rely on unions for training and benefits. Strategic segmentation of talent management is a major change for many organizations; it requires a well-articulated strategic message and strong leadership on the part of HR and the senior management leadership team.

ONBOARDING AND RETAINING TALENT

An organization's talent development principles should be obvious to job candidates at the time of hiring. As noted, most organizations need to offer multiple employee development arrangements that are strategy driven. These can range from almost guaranteed lifetime employment with continued development and growth opportunities to short-term, no-training, and no-employment-guarantee deals. The key is making it clear to all potential and existing employees what the arrangement is for them. The arrangement does not have to be a permanent one; it can change, and talent may move to a new arrangement after hiring. Further, the arrangement can change based on the needs and skills of talent, and the needs of the organization, but it is important that at all times individuals know what their current talent development arrangement is and what they can count on from the organization.

A leader in making its talent arrangements clear to employees is Netflix, which has an extensive website that makes it very clear to employees what the development model is. Most of Netflix's employees are covered by a model that places most of the responsibility for development on the employees and gives them no guarantee of a job or of further development. It does not feel it can guarantee long-term employment or a career with the organization, but on the other hand, it offers employees interesting work and high pay. The reason for this is that Netflix's business is changing rapidly (it has gone from merely renting DVDs to streaming and producing content) and the company does not feel it can make a reasonable long-term commitment to either employment or to developing the skills individuals need to be successful in the future. What Netflix can commit to is telling individuals where it thinks the business is going and what the key skill and talent issues are likely to be in the future.

The Netflix model fits the industry that the company is in: entertainment, an industry that is always and increasingly changing. Thus Netflix is, in many ways, just reflecting the realities of the business world it faces. It has a business strategy and talent development strategy that fits the rapidly changing environment it is in and the kind of technology and management skills it needs to be successful.

The onboarding process can only go so far in terms of getting the right retention message to talent, but it is the right stage at which to take a first step. From the beginning, employees should be given a clear message about what kind of future they can expect. This is particularly important for talent that makes a difference in organizational performance. These employees should receive a clear indication of the organization's commitment to their development and be given promises of regular ongoing career advice and encouragement. Employees who are not seen as pivotal or making a significant performance difference should be given a clear commitment concerning how they will be treated as long as they are with the organization. For example, an organization can say to them that they will be fairly paid and rewarded as long as they are needed by the organization and perform well. They also can be promised that they will be told as soon as possible about any changes that will affect their employment status.

Of course, a strong onboarding program is not a substitute for the ongoing, day-to-day, effective management of talent, but it is the critical first step in establishing the kind of relationship that an organization needs to have with its employees. The onboarding process should begin before the individual is actually hired, and a realistic job preview should be the first step in the process. Once individuals join the organization, it is time to further develop their understanding of what career options are available, make sure that they know how to get career advice and input, and provide an environment that has meaningful and appropriate development opportunities.

All supervisors should be trained and rewarded for their work on developing and retaining individuals. All too often this behavior is not measured and rewarded, and as a result managers do not do what they can and should to coach, direct, and develop their talent.

One key determinant of onboarding success is the initial work environment that employees enter. It is important that key employees, in particular, enter a positive work environment. Placing them in the right group with the right supervisor is a key step in their development and retention.

One thing that can help individuals get on board in a way that avoids early turnover is to put them in a socially friendly group. This can be a virtual group or a company-sponsored in-person socialization group that helps them feel a part of the organization and can give answers to their questions. A lot of early turnover of talent is a result of individuals not making any social connections and thus not feeling they are a part of the organization's social network and relationships.

TARGET TALENT DEVELOPMENT

Developing most skills is costly: training time is lost production time, and trainers are expensive, so it is often not a good investment to train people when others with comparable skills can be obtained in the labor market. Even if hiring a skilled individual from the outside requires a somewhat higher salary, it can often be less expensive from a total cost point of view to hire a skilled individual than to train someone. There are advantages to organization-supported development that have been demonstrated, including increased loyalty to the organization and increased retention of employees; but often in today's environment these advantages are outweighed by the costs associated with developing and training individuals who are already with the organization.

One alternative to company development programs is the use of Internet-based training and development programs. CrossKnowledge and Lynda.com are among the many vendors that provide organizations with programming that is targeted at developing employees. Organizations can make development available to individuals and allow them to self-develop. With this approach, organizations do not have to direct individual talent development or promise anything as a result of it occurring. Thus, it is a low-cost, low-risk development activity that may pay off if it leads to individuals acquiring the right skills. It may also make working for the organizations more attractive and less "risky" because of the development that is available.

It often makes sense to base development decisions on an individual's performance, but not to target only or primarily poor performers. It should be a meaningful reward for good performance and targeted at talent that wants to develop. In any case, before a commitment to skills development is made, it is important to analyze whether it is worth the cost. When an employee is performing poorly, particularly in an important position, the best solution is often replacement. Investment in training and development can be costly and may only lead to slower performance improvement than could be achieved by talent replacement.

Overall there are exceptions, but in most cases if a skill set can be obtained by recruiting somebody new, it is better to proceed in that direction than to train and develop an existing employee. This does not mean that organizations in today's and tomorrow's environment should not have some career paths that include training and development opportunities. There are skills for which it may make sense for an organization to build a career development approach, but these are becoming increasingly rare. It is generally true only for skills that are unique to the organization.

When an organization has a technology leadership position in a particular area, it makes sense to focus on skill development. There also may be operational approaches that organizations take with respect to management and customer relations that are unique and provide a competitive advantage. Developing these skills in talent is important because they cannot be obtained by getting someone from the job market and they provide a competitive advantage.

Finally, it is important for organizations to remember that development can be a great talent retention tool. Due to expense, it might not be the right tool for employees whose relationship to the organization is for the short term, but for situations where retention is a key issue (e.g., work and skills that make a difference) development can be a powerful retention device.

CAREER MODELS AND AGILITY

Once an organization has identified the skills it needs, the potential labor market for those skills, and where the organization stands with respect to its ability to gain a competitive advantage, it can develop the correct career and talent development model (or models). Depending upon an organization's need for talent, the possible approaches it can use can range from what might be called an app or gig talent development model to a traditional commitment to employee development.

AT&T is a good example of a company that has had to change its career and talent development models. As mentioned earlier, AT&T was once an exemplar of best practices with respect to career development; it used a model that fit the slowly changing, regulated phone business. But today it operates in a rapidly changing communications industry. It still talks to talent about careers, but stresses that individuals must own their development and continuously develop themselves. AT&T supports development by offering financial support for online degrees, so-called nanodegrees (individual online certifications), and individual courses. It has also made an effort to identify the skills it will need in the future and to make existing employees aware of what those skills will be.

Organizations that face very rapidly changing work environments, need skills that are relatively available, and have few skills that make a significant difference in their performance are strong candidates for temporary, contract, and gig employment relationships. Some organizations facing this situation have used a tour-of-duty relationship that is characterized by no commitment to long-term employment and little employee development but full-time employee status for as long as the "tour" lasts.

Gig and tour-of-duty organizations need some core individuals who maintain the culture and norms of the organization and develop the long-term strategy of the business. But the bulk of their employees have an employment deal that keeps them as long as they have the right skills and are needed for the operations that the organization engages in.

In a gig or tour-of-duty organization, who are likely to be the critical employees? Typically, they are the senior managers who are working on the long-term strategy and survivability of the organization and any employees that are doing things that are uniquely important to the organization's product development and delivery activities. The career talent development model for individuals who are doing important, high-value-added work should include long-term employment deals and development opportunities. Such an employment and career development relationship may look very much like the old General Electric and IBM models or perhaps the newer AT&T model. These individuals are likely to be a very small percentage of the total employees in an organization, and they are likely to be the most expensive employees because of the cost of their development. In comparison, most of the employees will have relatively low talent costs because of low development expense and little focus on talent retention.

What organizations fit into the gig/tour-of-duty category? Certainly organizations that actually provide temporary labor to other organizations and those that offer many services fit in this category. They include temporary employment agencies like Upwork, as well as on-call service firms such as Uber. These organizations keep their development costs at a minimum by simply making available a platform for individuals to make deals with customers for their services. In the case of gig work, there is the legal issue of whether the talent should be treated as employees of the company; but even if they are employees, which in many cases they are not, it does not make sense for the employer to invest heavily in their development. Other types of organizations that use the tour-of-duty model include firms that develop and utilize rapidly changing technologies, do project work or construction work, are in the entertainment industry, or offer seasonal services.

One way to think about the different types of talent development models is to contrast what the organizations that adopt them look like. With a traditional model, most individuals are long-term employees whom the organization is willing to invest in and develop. With the gig model, there is a small number of core employees, and the organization invests in their skills, but it depends on gig or contract employees to do most of the work. Both of these models are potentially effective approaches to career and talent development—as, of course, are multiple intermediary models. The key strategy issue is finding the right combination of talent development practices so that an organization can achieve a competitive advantage that is based on one or more of the following capabilities: agility, speed, technical knowledge, cost, and product quality.

RETAINING TALENT

A major issue in talent development is talent retention. Turnover is expensive from an administrative and development point of view, but its greatest expense often is the productivity of the talent that is lost. Of course, there is enormous variance in the value of talent. In some cases there may be little lost value because the individual who leaves does not have skills, abilities, or performance levels that are difficult to find in the labor market. On the other hand, if the individual had unique skills and a high level of performance, that loss of talent may be extremely costly. The implications of the costs that are associated with talent retention and loss are clear. Organizations need to carefully monitor the cost of replacing their talent and behave accordingly—that is, they need to do everything they can to retain individuals for whom the cost of replacement is high.

There is an enormous amount of theory and research on why individuals leave organizations. It starts with the basic point that job satisfaction is strongly related to turnover—unhappy employees leave, and happy employees stay. This raises the issue of what makes employees happy. There is a large body of research on this that shows that there is no one thing that determines satisfaction, but it is possible to identify some key factors. These include the nature of the work employees are doing, the rewards they receive, and how they are treated by their supervisors. It also is influenced by the type of career and development opportunities that employees are offered. The opportunity to develop and progress in an organization can be a powerful satisfaction and retention factor.

A very high percentage of employees leave their jobs before they have spent a year with an organization. This varies widely, of course, by organization and type of job. It can be 70 percent or higher, but rarely is it much lower than 25 percent. This high early turnover is a result of many factors, and seems to be increasing as a result of the attitudes of younger workers with respect to their careers. They expect to hold many jobs in their lifetime, and see no problem in changing jobs every two to three years. Of course, short tenure may not always be a problem for an organization, depending on the skills that the individuals have and the ease of replacing them. But in the case of key hard-to-replace talent, the turnover of employees—and especially new ones—is very expensive.

There is little organizations can do about job offers their employees receive from other organizations, but there is a great deal they can do about how their employees are treated and therefore how satisfied they are. As is stressed throughout this chapter, those who have key skills need to be treated very well relative to the market. What does this mean? It means that they need to be rewarded well above market levels so that it is highly unlikely they will be offered a better situation somewhere else. The same does not necessarily hold true for other employees, however, and this may lead to issues of perceived internal inequity. This is an inevitable consequence of strategically targeting skills and talent, a necessity in a talent economy. It should be explained to all talent as being strategy driven.

To identify individuals who are likely to leave, it is important that organizations undertake regular attitude surveys that measure engagement and satisfaction. As most surveys are anonymous, they typically do not indicate which individuals are likely candidates for departure, but they can indicate areas and critical skill groups within the organization that are in danger of losing employees. Frequent short online "pulse" surveys can and should be used to track satisfaction and identify actions that are needed. Action then needs to be taken based on the results, and there needs to be a clear link between the survey results and the actions.

Some organizations have found that they can predict turnover by looking at factors other than job satisfaction—for example, the kind of Internet activity that employees engage in. Looking at job websites, being active on LinkedIn, or certain postings on social media forums may indicate that employees are thinking about leaving the organization. Other indicators may be their attendance behavior and their performance. This is an area where the use of analytics and segmentation can pay big dividends.

Overall it makes a great deal of sense to monitor the behavior and attitudes of all talent, but particularly key talent, to determine whether it is likely to leave the organization. Obviously, when it is determined that turnover is likely, steps need to be taken to retain key individuals and groups—particularly those that have critical skills. In short, organizations need a targeted retention system that includes indicators of potential turnover and corrective actions to be taken.

HUMAN CAPITAL REPORTING

As already noted, human capital is an increasingly important organizational asset; in many cases, it is an organization's most important asset. It should therefore be at the forefront of the minds and agendas of all managers, just like the financial assets and physical assets of every organization are. Yet, sadly, it is not. Managers and the public regularly get reports on the condition of the financial and physical assets of organizations. These are publicly reported, and the reports are audited by independent accounting firms. On the other hand, most organizations report very little to their employees, shareholders, and the public on the condition of their human capital and how it is treated.

In the past several decades there has been an increase in the number of organizations conducting surveys to find out the attitudes of employees. The results of these surveys are usually not made public, and they are inconsistently used as levers for change in organizations. All too often the best information on how talent is treated by an organization can be found on websites like Glassdoor that survey employees and post the results.

For talent to be effectively managed, valid talent measurement systems need to be in place. Things that get measured get attended to; things that are not measured do not. Further, those things that are measured and publicly reported typically get more attention than those things that are measured but the results of which are kept private. Thus, in an era where talent is very important to organizations, it is increasingly critical that organizations measure the condition of their talent and report it both internally and to shareholders.

At the very least, an organization should internally report on such obvious human capital indicators as turnover, absenteeism, satisfaction, engagement, and money spent on training and development, and the results should be made known to everyone in the organization. In addition, managers should be held accountable for the results in their areas of supervision and rewarded based on those results.

A number of efforts have been made to develop public reporting practices with respect to corporate talent management and development. The annual reports of some companies occasionally provide limited information on the condition of their talent. Several groups have developed standards for reporting costs and activity levels in areas such as training, development, absenteeism, and turnover, but at the moment there is no generally accepted standard way of reporting these data to investors and the public. As a result, organizations say that human capital is their most important asset, but shareholders, executives, and managers typically get little if any data about the condition of this vital asset. This clearly needs to change, and in major and important ways. Organizations need to report on the condition of their human capital and on the costs associated with the management of that capital. Further, managers need to be held accountable for how they perform with respect to the development of human capital. Only if this happens will talent management get the focus that it deserves in the new world of work.

CONCLUSION

The talent development practices of organizations should be driven by their business strategy and the skills needed to successfully execute it. As noted in table 5.1, the key is using the business strategy to determine the kind of talent attraction and development that occurs, as well as the kind of employment deals and contracts that organizations have with their talent. In most cases a strategy-driven talent development approach will lead to organizations having multiple career and development models. In these segmented approaches, some employees will receive virtually no development while others may receive extensive, long-term development support. Some will be full-time employees, while others may be part-time or gig employees.

In most cases, individuals who have key skills need to be full-time employees of an organization, and in many cases they should have a

Table 5.1 Developing talent

Strategy driven	Target key talent; develop mix of employment deals that fit strategy
Skills based	Focus on developing and retaining key skills
Performance focused	Reward and retain based on skills and performance
Agile	Structure employment deals and employee development to fit the need for agility
Segmented	Develop and create work relationships based on skills needed
Evidence based	Analyze costs and benefits of development; assess engagement and turnover of talent

long-term employment deal. They should have employment that is dependent on their performance and they should be rewarded in ways that retain them and motivate them to develop their skills. For individuals who do not have key skills, multiple models may be appropriate. They may be in positions with little development and low job security but hold full-time status. Alternatively, they may be gig employees who have only transactional relationships with their organizations.

Agility needs to be a major determinant of the type of attraction, development, and retention that organizations practice. The more agile an organization needs to be, the more it needs to make difficult decisions about whether to train and develop employees to deal with the changes it needs to make or to deal with those changes by replacing certain members of the workforce so that it can maintain or improve its performance and capabilities. Obviously, those organizations that decide they need to be agile but cannot successfully retrain their workforce because of cost, speed, or other reasons need to take a very limited and targeted approach to talent development. They need to become experts in how to fill jobs by going to the labor market.

In today's world, most organizations should have significantly segmented workforces. In terms of attracting talent this means that employment deals will vary from little or no development to extensive investments in individual growth and development. The key issue is making sure that the right skills and individuals are chosen for development and that retention is a strong focus for those individuals who are being developed.

It is hard to see how talent development and retention in an organization can work well in the absence of evidence concerning the effectiveness of recruiting, development, and retention efforts. The key is the development and commitment of the right individuals. Doing this on an organization-wide basis requires cost and effectiveness data with respect to recruiting, developing, and retaining talent. Cost data are particularly needed with respect to making good decisions about whether development is the best choice. This analysis requires considerable data and careful measurement, but it needs to be done; it is the foundation upon which talent development should be built.

There is also the issue of how effective talent development programs are. Many organizations spend millions of dollars on development without solid data indicating what the costs and benefits are of these programs. Good decision making about talent development requires good evidence about what works and what does not, how much it costs, and how it does or does not support the business strategy of the organization.

6

REWARDING TALENT

The reward systems in most organizations do not focus on skills and competencies, business strategy, team and organization performance, or the differences that exist in the workforce with respect to what individuals want, need, and value. Instead they still follow a traditional bureaucratic model and are based on job evaluation systems, merit pay, and a fixed set of fringe benefits. These reward systems are usually the same for most or all hourly employees. Salaried workers, executives, and perhaps salespeople usually have plans that are based on job evaluations and include merit pay raises and benefits. In some organizations these plans include stock, profit sharing, and the giving of bonuses. Overall, however, most reward systems fail to focus on the key issues of today's work environment.

How do reward systems need to be designed to fit the organizations and individuals that operate in the new world of work? The answer is obvious: they need to focus on the skills and competencies individuals have, on the contributions that they make to improving organizational performance, and on the needs, desires, and preferences of employees for cash and noncash compensation. To accomplish this, a reward system needs to adopt a number of practices that have not yet gained widespread acceptance and adoption.

PAY FOR SKILLS, NOT JOBS

The predominant compensation approach in corporations dictates that individuals are paid primarily based upon the hierarchical level and nature of the job they hold and its market rate. The key tool in this approach is an evaluation system that scores jobs on a scale of measurement that examines job attributes. With this methodology and salary surveys, the amount paid to particular positions within an organization can be compared with the pay in other organizations.

The problem with basing pay on jobs is that it is individuals, not jobs, that have a value in the labor market. It follows from this that the best way to attract, retain, and motivate skilled talent is to base pay on the skills they have. Today most organizations do pay some individuals based on the skills they have, but this practice is still the exception rather than the rule. For example, some knowledge workers are paid based on the kind of skills they have, but in many cases these individuals are not paid based upon their individual levels of their expertise but on the *type* of expertise they have. In many areas, including finance, accounting, engineering, and human resources, and certainly in areas like software and various areas of research and development, individuals should be paid based on the kind and level of expertise they have that is relevant to the work they do.

Some organizations target their pay rates above market levels, others pay at market levels, and others pay below market though they rarely say so publicly. Missing altogether or playing only a minor role in this approach to determining pay is a focus on the skills and knowledge that are critical to an individual's work performance and incentives for individuals to develop and improve those skills and knowledge. Instead, they are incentivized to move on to more highly evaluated jobs because that is the way they can get a pay increase.

The movement of Procter & Gamble and other corporations toward self-managing teams in their high involvement management plants, which began in the 1960s, led to the limited adoption of paying people for their skills. These high-involvement workplaces paid individuals based primarily on the number and kind of skills that they had, not on the jobs they were doing at a specific point in time. This encouraged these individuals to develop a broader understanding of the work processes, to become more flexible, and to improve their skills. It was a significant step toward establishing the effectiveness of skills-based pay, and it showed that it can replace traditional job evaluation–based pay with a more effective approach that contributes directly to organizational effectiveness.

The next step should be the movement of all organizations toward paying most, if not all, of their talent for the market value of the skills they have that are relevant to the organization's work and strategy. A skills- and knowledge-based system is an excellent way to motivate talent to learn new, critical skills and to help attract and retain individuals with the right skill sets. Because talent, not a job, has value, it can provide a valuable tool for attracting and developing the kind of talent organizations need to be competitive in knowledge-based businesses.

A skills- and knowledge-based pay system creates the opportunity to compensate the most valuable individuals above market levels and to encourage people in the organization to master those skills that are major determinants of an organization's effectiveness. This is a key element in creating a talent management system that supports an organization's strategic agenda and agility. For this very reason technology companies including GoDaddy, Google, and Netflix are increasingly adopting this approach, particularly with respect to their knowledge workers. They determine what their talent is paid by looking at what the market pays for individuals with the same or similar skills. For example, individuals are paid based on multiple levels of software skills that are priced according to the market.

Adopting a skills- and knowledge-based pay system is increasingly feasible. More and more data exist on what individuals with particular skill sets are paid. And with modern information technology, skill assessment is easier and more effective than ever before. Further, paying for skills is directly tied to the need for organizations to emphasize agility, develop talent with key skills, and position people as a source of competitive advantage.

There are some key operational issues that appear when organizations move to a skills- and knowledge-based reward system. For example, decisions need to be made about which employees can learn and develop certain skills and eventually whether they have mastered them. There are no easy answers to these issues, but as we will see in chapter 7, they need to be part of the ongoing performance management discussions that take place with individuals about their careers and their value to the organization.

An organization that pays for skills and knowledge needs to make clear statements about when and how decisions will be made about opportunities to learn new skills and acquire new knowledge. Organizations also need to be very clear about which skills they need and are willing to pay individuals for having. It makes no sense to simply reward individuals for acquiring what are strategically irrelevant skills given their position in the organization. A second component that needs to be in place for an effective skills-based system to operate is valid measurement of whether an individual has acquired particular skills and competencies. How this will be done needs to be made clear in advance, particularly when individuals contract to learn a new skill.

Finally, there is the issue of what happens when an organization no longer needs a particular skill set. In today's rapidly changing environment, this can happen with technical and many other types of skills. The best approach here is to let individuals know that the skill (or skills) they are being paid for is no longer needed in the organization and to give them a window of time to replace it with a new skill that is needed. If they fail to replace it, their pay is reduced because they no longer have the skills that justify their current pay rate.

One pay-for-skills option that can be used in some situations is giving individuals a bonus, one-time recognition, or other reward for learning a new skill. This is particularly appropriate when an individual's base pay is already relatively high compared to the market and where a pay increase will put him or her significantly above market levels. Rather than putting the individual into a situation where the salary cost of employment is excessive, he or she can be offered a one-time cash bonus, stock in the company, or some other reward for learning an additional skill or a new capability.

Given that the nature of work is changing rapidly and new skills need to be learned or acquired in a relatively short period of time, a focus on paying talent based on what it can do is the best approach because it rewards and motivates skills development. In some cases it is less expensive, and in many cases it is more effective than replacing individuals with new talent that possesses the desired skills. This is particularly likely when the learning time for the needed skills is not long or the market (and market price) for talent with the skills is very high.

Paying for skills fits well with how the gig- or talent-demand economy operates: this economy is very much based on paying for what someone can do. Thus, when decisions are being made about how to get work done (e.g., gig work versus employee work), it makes a direct comparison much easier.

Yes, paying for skills is a big change, but it is the approach that is needed to move from a bureaucratic job description–based world to the skills- and competencies-based world of agile, effective organizations. It must happen if organizations hope to change and to motivate individuals to develop the right skills. It also allows an organization to pay people in a way that is consistent with the idea that there are certain key skills that need to be rewarded and retained. Paying more for these key skills is a very effective way to accomplish this.

The market for talent is increasingly becoming a skills-based one. It is no longer primarily a job-based market, and the most effective way for an organization to attract and retain individuals who have the strategically important skills it needs (or *any* skills, for that matter) is to base their rewards on what they can do and what the organization needs them to do rather than base them on what other organizations pay people for doing similar jobs.

MARKET POSITION

Simply stated, having high reward levels relative to the market can pay off for an organization, particularly when it is done for performance and skills that are pivotal. Why? It aids the attraction and retention of all talent, but particularly key talent. Pay and other rewards are key to individuals being attracted to and satisfied with how they are treated by an organization. Therefore, it will contribute to a low turnover and a positive buzz about what the organization is like as an employer. Of course, it is not the only thing that attracts and retains employees, but it is hard for an organization to present itself as an attractive employer when it is absent. Yes, organizations can emphasize their social purpose and mission, and in some cases this can make up for having a pay and rewards position that is at or below the market level, but this appeals to only a limited number of people and can be a difficult position for many organizations to argue.

The key issue with paying above the market rate, of course, is the cost. Can it be justified? Frequently it can be if it reduces turnover and attracts a better quality workforce. But there is an additional consideration:

whether an organization expects and demands above-market performance from its employees. If it does this by terminating those individuals who are below market in their performance and skills, it is an effective approach to determining where the pay and rewards levels are set in an organization.

Netflix is a good example of an organization that has a high-pay, high-performance culture. The company makes it very clear that individuals who do not perform above the market level will not continue to be employed. It also makes it clear to its talent that it pays above-market wages with the expectation of performance that is also above market. This gives Netflix the advantage of legitimately being able to set high goals for individuals and having credibility when it removes average and below-average performers. It also attracts individuals who have self-confidence and believe that they are high performers.

In a pay system where the amount of pay is based on the skills individuals have, it is important to allow for and enable adjustments in pay when individuals learn new skills and when the market for their skills changes. This may mean more than an annual change in an individual's pay. At the very least, all individuals should be reviewed every year—and in the case of key talent, every quarter—to be sure that their pay level is at the appropriate market position. If it is below market, they should be granted a salary increase to bring them up to whatever position in the market has been targeted for the skills they have. As noted already, in most cases this means an above-market position. If the market for their skills has actually decreased, they should be given a freeze notice rather than a pay decrease. This means that their pay will not be moved up unless and until the market for their skills moves above what they are currently being paid.

PERFORMANCE-BASED REWARDS

The evidence is clear: basing rewards on performance can be a powerful motivator of performance. Rewarding performance is not only an effective motivator of performance, it is a way to attract and retain the best performers. In order to motivate performance, rewards need to be clearly connected to performance, and they need to be important. Frequently organizations try to accomplish this by giving the highest salary increases to their best performers and through the use of profit-sharing plans, stock plans, and bonuses. Organizations also sometimes create a variety of recognition programs that reward performance. All of these are viable ways to create a meaningful connection between pay and performance, but vary greatly in their effectiveness.

The least effective way to reward performance using financial incentives is to give "merit" salary increases; it also is the method most frequently used. Among the reasons for its low effectiveness is that the amount of money available tends to be very much determined by inflation, not performance. As a result, in many time periods the salary increase budget is so small that it is impossible to create a meaningful reward difference between good performers and poor performers. Simply stated, a 3 percent merit budget is hard to divide up in ways that leads good performers to feel they have received significantly more than lower-level performers.

Profit sharing and stock ownership plans can have a positive impact on talent performance, attraction, and retention. They will not work for all talent, but they will for most. With respect to performance, the impact of profit sharing plans on talent motivation is likely to be minor unless the amount received can be tied directly to an individual's or small group's performance. The problem is that most individuals do not see a clear connection between their performance and their reward amount when it is based on organization performance. This problem is even greater for stock ownership plans. However, like profit sharing plans, they can help create a culture of involvement, attraction, and retention if they lead to above-market compensation levels.

What is needed for a pay plan to have a major impact on motivation is a bonus plan that has a level of funding and a measurement approach that allows it to make a difference of at least 9 percent between what good performance earns and what poor performance earns. The amount of bonus can be determined by a budgeted amount or triggered by various levels and kinds of organizational effectiveness—for example, company profit.

Driving the amount of money in a bonus plan off organizational performance has a number of advantages, including causing talent to focus not only on their individual performance but also on organizational performance. The negative in this approach is that when individuals perform well but the organization does not, even the good performers will receive little or no bonus. As a result, they may see little connection between their performance and their reward.

The right mix of individually determined and collectively determined rewards is very situational; there is no answer that is always best. A careful analysis is needed of the organization's business model and the degree to which individuals are best focused on their own performance, on the organization's performance, and on how volatile the organization's overall results are likely to be. What needs to be true, in almost all bonus periods, is that there is money available, and individuals who perform well get a significant bonus at the end of the period.

There are some conditions under which paying for performance makes sense for temporary, short-term, contract, and gig employees. If they have a carefully prescribed task to perform with measureable outcomes, a very strong case can be made for rewarding them based on their performance. Since in most cases they have no chance at being given a full-time job or being rewarded in other ways for their performance, offering them a financial incentive that is based on their performance fits a need and makes a great deal of sense. What kind of financial incentive is appropriate? The answer in most cases is cash, since it has a universal high value.

In the case of most nonemployee talent, cash rewards should be based on individual performance. There are some situations where a group incentive is appropriate—primarily those where a cooperative group task is involved and performance is best or only measurable at the group level. In any case, it should be an immediate reward clearly tied to measurable performance during the time nonemployees are doing work for the organization. It is important that the nature of the deal be presented to the individuals when they agree to do the work. They should also be given ongoing feedback on how well they are performing relative to their opportunity to earn a reward.

One additional note. In some cases it may be particularly important for temporary or short-term workers to have an incentive to perform well. In cases where they are paid on an hourly basis, the incentive for them is in the direction of performing slowly or in a "reserved" manner. The major reason is that once these individuals finish their gig, they may be out of work because they do not have another gig lined up. As a result, rather than being motivated to perform well, they are motivated to perform at the lowest possible level of productivity that they can get away with to prolong their work relationship. Pay for performance can motivate them to perform more rapidly. It is not an "everything" solution, but it can bring an important motivator into play for employees that are not regular employees of the organization.

Overall, the most generally applicable approach to paying talent for performance is some combination of a budgeted bonus plan that rewards individual performance and a business unit or a corporate performance–funded bonus plan like profit sharing. These two approaches to paying for performance should be designed to operate relatively independently, so that if the organization does not do well, individuals who perform well can be rewarded based on the money put aside for individual bonuses.

Bonuses for individuals should not replace market adjustments to base pay; they should be paid out based on performance, not market movement. The combination of market and performance pay gives individuals the chance to increase their base pay because of changes in the market and/or in their skills, and to receive a bonus or merit salary increase based on their individual performance. This design has the advantage of creating a performance focus on the part of individuals because it provides a high level of assurance that if they perform well, they will be rewarded for it. It also has the advantage of keeping the pay of an organization's talent in line with the market so there is no threat of losing them for pay reasons.

REWARD SEGMENTATION AND CHOICE

Many organizations give different kinds of rewards to individuals at different levels in the hierarchy and in different types of jobs. For example, senior executives often receive stock and very different benefits from those given to lower-level employees. In the 1970s some organizations began using flexible or "cafeteria" style benefit plans that offered all employees a choice of what "fringe" benefits they receive. In these plans, individuals are given a "budget" and allowed to "buy" the benefits they want.

Recently, a number of companies have taken the reward choice idea to interesting new levels. First, they have increased the benefits and perks they offer to job holders. Today, particularly in Silicon Valley and in technology firms in general, employees can choose to have concierge services, extra vacation days, engage in various kinds of on-site physical exercise (Ping-Pong is popular in Silicon Valley firms), partake of entertainment, and go to a cafeteria with many food options. The reality is that individuals value rewards differently, and that to optimize the return on the investment organizations make in them, it makes sense to try to match the rewards to the preferences of individuals. In the absence of this, organizations may give individuals rewards (fringe benefits, in particular) that are valued at a level that is below their cost—not a good way to spend compensation money.

The key point here is that individuals increasingly differ in what they value and what they want. As a result, choice is a winner; it helps assure that what organizations give to individuals are things that they want and value.

Admittedly, choice can go too far and organizations can end up attracting and retaining individuals for the wrong reasons or spending more than they need to because they give things or amounts that are not important when it comes to the attraction, retention, and performance of talent. This is particularly true in cases where individuals are given various kinds of recreation and off-the-job benefits that are not performance-based rewards and do not add to their ability to perform their work. Indeed, they may distract individuals from doing their jobs and developing their job-related skills. Admittedly, they may help attract and retain some talent, but it may not be the right talent, and the price may be too high. This is particularly true when the benefits are available to all employees at no cost. Unlike flexible benefit plans, in these plans, often there is no limit placed on how many services and options individuals can choose, and no trade-off choices need be made.

The answer to the effectiveness question with respect to most non-financial benefits can only be determined by analyzing usage, retention, and performance data. Now that so much data exist and can be analyzed, it is possible to make evidence-based decisions about the effectiveness of most reward programs. Some reward preference data can be gathered using opinion surveys and other tools that indicate employees' preferences for different kinds of rewards. In most cases, however, the best data on preferences and the best way to ensure that the rewards chosen are the right ones comes from giving individuals a choice of rewards. If they have a choice that includes cash, they will consistently pick benefits that have a high value to them, and as a result, the organization will receive a good return on its reward costs.

What should not be lost in the fascination with nontraditional benefits, and the changes that are occurring in the kinds of rewards some organizations are offering today, is that members of the workforce differ dramatically in what they value and what attracts and retains them. This fundamental point means that organizations cannot rely on a relatively small number of reward types and that they need to allow individuals to determine what they receive in order to get full value for the cost of the rewards. Putting together a package of rewards that most or all individuals will value, at or above cost, is becoming an increasingly complex task. Thus, a limited predetermined set of rewards for individuals is becoming less and less the way to operate. It is simply not likely to produce a high "hit" rate and a good return on the cost of the rewards.

Finally, it is important for organizations to determine which rewards attract and retain the right employees. It may be that retention can be improved by offering Ping-Pong and dry cleaning, but who does it attract and retain? Is it the most cost-effective way to retain the best performers? Little research exists that answers these questions. In most cases, they are best answered by organizations using analytics and research evidence that focuses on their workforce and looks at how effective different rewards are at attracting and retaining talent.

PUBLIC PAY

Most organizations keep the pay levels of many of their employees secret. There is, however, a growing trend toward making pay data public. Many organizations now give out the pay ranges for jobs and the ranges for bonuses, but the pay of most individuals is still kept secret in most private sector organizations in the Americas, Asia, and Europe.

There are a number of arguments in favor of secrecy. According to traditional wisdom, it prevents comparisons that are disturbing to individuals, protects rights of privacy, and in general leads to more effective pay administration because decision makers do not have to be worried about negative reactions to their decisions.

There is no doubt that keeping pay secret does prevent some disruptions that might occur if pay information were public knowledge. It makes it impossible for individuals to see whether they are paid more or less than others whom they may think are less—or for that matter, more—deserving. But it also allows age, race, and gender discrimination to go unmonitored, and it makes it impossible for individuals to know whether they and others are paid according to company policy. It is one thing for an organization to say that pay is based on performance; it is quite another for its members to be able to see that it is. Finally, secrecy makes it impossible to hold managers and organizations accountable for their decisions regarding pay, and as a result, they often make worse decisions than they would make if they were held publically accountable.

Overall, there are good reasons to believe that public disclosure of pay rates will lead to pay being more fairly administered and to a positive impact in the workplace. My research shows that with secrecy, individuals misperceive what others make. In general, they tend to overestimate the pay of individuals at their level and as a result they feel their own pay is lower relative to others than it actually is. The result is lower motivation, more dissatisfaction, and a greater risk of turnover.

Secrecy can make it less clear that a strong positive relationship between pay and performance exists and as a result, can decrease the motivation of individuals. Of course, in all too many cases, pay is not tied to performance and thus making pay public will just prove to employees that there is no relationship. The answer here is to create the connection and make it public. It is not—as is often done in organizations that practice secrecy—saying there is such a connection when in fact there is none and hoping that it will be believed.

Slowly but surely, pay information is being made public by organizations, but the movement is far too slow. A wild card with respect to making pay public are employment review websites like Glassdoor, which put pay data that is given to them by employees into the public domain. The problem with Glassdoor and similar sites making pay rates public is that they may not have accurate or complete data, and therefore, what is made public ends up hurting an organization more than if the organization itself made its actual pay data public.

For decades I have advised organizations to make pay public, and they frequently agree with the idea, but they typically point out that they need a "few years" to get their organization's pay system and rates to where they feel comfortable making them public (secrecy tends to lead to indefensible decisions). The problem is that when I check in with them after those "few years" have passed, they typically have not made the improvements that are needed to have defensible pay rates and, as a result, making pay public is delayed further. The reason for this is what caused the pay system to get to an indefensible position in the first place: with secrecy, an organization is not and cannot be held accountable by employees for its pay decisions.

Recently, the growing diversity of the workforce has raised an increasing number of questions about the fairness of pay and the tendency for women and minorities to be paid less than white men. It is suspected and often true, but it is hard for individuals to challenge most pay decisions because they do not have data to support their claims. This has led to more demands that pay be made public so clarity can be developed about the pay practices of organizations and about the treatment of women and minorities. The proliferation of pay information on social media forums may be an indicator that many younger individuals do not support pay secrecy and that in the future there will be more public pressure to make pay information public.

There is an increasing amount of legislation in the United States that requires some pay information to be made public. It is likely that this trend will continue. Although it may not go as far as organizations being required to make the pay of their individual employees public, this may eventually happen, just as it happened decades ago for top executives and has happened for all employees in some countries.

One final issue with respect to pay secrecy is the hacking of company computer systems and the potential it has to make pay information public. This is just what happened to Sony when its salary database in the United States was hacked by the North Korean government.

At this point it seems safe to assume that any organization's pay data can be hacked and made public. What should organizations do about this? They can, of course, install greater cybersecurity, but there is a better, simpler alternative: make pay public and administer it in a way that is defensible. This is more likely to increase organizational effectiveness and to cost less in the long run. Making pay public will improve performance if it shows a clear connection between pay and performance, since this will actually end up motivating individuals to improve their skills and perform better. Overall, making pay and reward practices public is potentially a win-win situation if an organization has reasonable, defensible, and strategically aligned pay policies and reward practices.

CONCLUSION

Traditional reward system practices do not fit well in organizations built for the new world of work. As table 6.1 shows, practices need to be much more strategic and more focused on keeping, attracting, and retaining individuals with the right skills. One way to accomplish this is to focus the base pay system of organizations on an individual's skill set. In this approach, individuals are paid for the skills they have that are relevant to their contribution to the organization's performance and strategy. To align a skills-based approach to pay with an organization's strategy, those skills that are strategically important should be more highly rewarded relative to the market than are less-important skills. The reason for this is simple: the retention and attraction of individuals with key skills is essential to implementing an organization's strategy.

Pay for performance should also be an important part of an organization's reward system. In most cases, today's and tomorrow's organizations should have systems that target both individual and collective

Table 6.1 Rewarding talent

Strategy driven	Target key skills for higher pay; Reward key performance
Skills based	Base pay rates on skills
Performance focused	Reward individual, team, and organization performance with bonuses and stock
Agile	Reward skill development to fit the need for agility
Segmented	Different amounts and kinds of rewards based on skills and performance; reward choices available
Evidence based	Analyze performance of individuals making different reward choices; analyze impact of rewards on performance, turnover, and attraction

performance with a multitude of rewards. Indeed, the kind and amount of rewards individuals get in most cases should reflect their choices and their individual work situations. Too often, given the diverse nature of today's workplace, the rewards that traditional organizations offer are not valued highly by a significant portion of the workforce relative to their cost. Choice and variety are the answer here, not steering away from rewarding performance.

The complex issues that are raised as a result of today's new workforce and workplaces very much require an evidence-based approach to rewards. Data need to be gathered about which rewards are attracting the right kind of employees, how effective rewards systems are in motivating performance, and the attraction and retention rates that are produced by various reward system practices. Given the dynamic nature of the workforce and workplace, evidence needs to be continuously gathered. Surveys and performance measures should be used to determine how effective the reward systems in organizations are at leading to strategy implementation and organizational performance.

7

PERFORMANCE MANAGEMENT

Performance management is one of the most important and potentially impactful talent management processes that organizations can use. Yet as it is currently designed and executed by most organizations, it is the most unpopular talent management process that organizations engage in. For decades, both appraisers and appraisees have voiced their unhappiness and have resisted and complained about performance appraisal programs that require annual performance evaluations and ratings.

It is easy to understand why traditional performance appraisals are disliked by both appraisers and appraisees. For decades they have been an annual activity that results in grades or ratings being given to each employee and an often uncomfortable meeting between a manager and a subordinate to discuss a performance rating and its consequences. Appraisals often take large amounts of preparation and execution time. They result in miscommunication and often disappointment when, as frequently occurs, the appraisal rating turns out to be lower than expected. Not surprisingly, they are almost always lower than expected because individuals tend to rate themselves more positively than do the supervisors rating them. Despite their unpopularity, most organizations continue to do performance appraisals on an annual basis.

In response to the perception and reality that appraisals waste time and are unpopular, a number of corporations (e.g., Accenture, Adobe, General Electric, and Sears) have made major changes to their appraisal systems while a few have eliminated appraisals entirely. Elimination reduces the pain and suffering, but does not meet the need of individuals and organizations to have valid measures of performance. Further, it does not give individuals the feedback and development advice they need to improve their performance.

Instead of simply eliminating all performance management activities, some organizations have correctly diagnosed the situation as one that needs attention and can be made better by executing performance management in an effective manner. The challenge is identifying what constitutes an effective process for a particular work situation and executing it.

Fortunately, there is a great deal of research evidence that indicates what performance management must look like and how it must be done in order to fit today's workplace. It indicates that performance reviews need to be undertaken in a very different manner than they have in the past and that when they are the results can be positive. There can be less wasted time, fewer hurt feelings, improved performance, and greater organizational effectiveness. For this to happen, there are a number of features that need to be part of the performance management process.

THE PROCESS SHOULD BE LED BY EXECUTIVES

The execution of an organization's strategy depends on people understanding what needs to be achieved (goals that fit with strategy), ongoing conversations that provide feedback, holding people accountable, helping them develop the skills to reach challenging goals, and providing meaningful and nuanced evaluations of the impact of what they do. This is what good performance management will accomplish. If top management does not support a disciplined rigorous process of performance management, organizations will not be able to deliver the results they want and need.

All too often an organization's human resources (HR) function is given the task of designing, implementing, advocating for, and operating the performance management system of the organization. HR representatives become policemen and -women as well as the designers of and the major advocates for the process. They spend a great deal of time to ensure it gets done, that the right distribution of evaluation scores exists, and so on. The perception that develops in organizations is that the appraisal process is both an HR process and a dysfunctional, bureaucratic one. It is not seen as a strategic driver that is intended to support the business strategy, motivate performance, and enable individuals to develop the right skill sets and careers.

To be perceived as an enabler of strategic performance, the performance management process needs to be driven and utilized by an organization's top executives; they need to advocate for it, implement it, use it with their direct reports, and experience it in their own roles. They also need to evaluate how well performance management is used by the managers who report to them, the managers that report to their subordinates, and so on—down through the organization. Unless there is a top-down commitment to doing it well and senior managers acting as role models of effective performance management behavior, there is little to no chance it will be a key driver of business strategy and taken seriously throughout the organization. Instead of performance management being an important asset, it is bound to become a bureaucratic process that is done poorly to fulfill an HR bureaucratic requirement. Indeed, in organizations that do not have senior management support for the process it is probably best not to conduct performance appraisals at all. Not doing them can save time and avoid the negative results that come from poorly executed appraisals.

What does senior management support look like when it comes to performance management? It starts with establishing and articulating the organization's goals and objectives and creating a good process for its execution. All senior managers need to support the process and evaluate their subordinates on how well they carry out the process. It needs to be a key indicator of how effective a manager is, and managers need to be trained in how they must behave in order for it to work effectively. It should be treated as a key skill set for managers: no one should be a manager if he or she cannot master performance management.

One of the major reasons why senior managers need to support and drive performance management is that there is every indication that it is a very effective driver of performance when it results in setting strategic goals and when the accomplishment of goals is part of the evaluation process. This means that senior managers need to both contribute to the goal-setting process and hold their subordinates responsible for meeting goals. This same approach needs to cascade down through the organization so that the goals are driven by the business strategy and are not simply something "nice to do." With this approach, generic and meaningless goals, which do not relate to behavior and cannot be evaluated fairly, do not get set.

THE PROCESS SHOULD NOT BE AN ANNUAL ONE

The performance review process in most organizations has been and continues to be an annual event. Every year, managers and subordinates sit down to review the performance of the subordinates; a score is given at the same time, or soon thereafter, and sometimes goals are set for next year. The problem with this type of calendar-driven event is that it does not fit the timing of the business processes and results of most organizations. It may have fit the old world of work but it does not fit the rate of change that exists today. In most cases, it creates too much time between goal setting and evaluation, and in a few cases it does not provide enough time.

Changes need to be made in how frequently performance discussions take place and feedback is given to individuals about their goal accomplishments. The same is true for setting new goals and having individuals respond to them. Perhaps the best way to characterize them is to say that the goal-setting and performance appraisal processes need to be on a schedule that depends on the nature of the work that someone is doing, not the calendar. This may lead to very different schedules for talent doing different types of work. That said, appraisals should as a general rule take place at least every quarter to fit the rate of change that exists today in most organizations and to support organizational agility.

In today's organizations, jobs differ enormously in what is sometimes called the "time span of discretion," which is how long it takes to see the impact of what employees do on their jobs. In the case of goal-driven systems, it refers to how long it takes for them to accomplish a goal that has been set for them. In practice, this can be a matter of a few minutes, but more likely it can span days, weeks, months, or maybe even years. To make performance reviews appropriate and timely, they need to be made to fit the time span of the work that individuals are doing. This can get rather complicated because individuals may have some goals that need to be appraised and feedback given after a relatively short period of time while other goals can only be appraised and judged over a longer period of time. Properly designed apps and programs that support goal setting, updating, and appraisal can help here.

At any point in time, every individual should have multiple active goals, a clear understanding of their expected completion dates, and an understanding of how goal accomplishment will be measured, scored, and rewarded. They should also know when they will need to meet with their appraiser or appraisers to discuss how they have performed relative to their goals. This type of dynamic performance management system is likely to involve many more meetings and more ongoing communication than the traditional annual meeting model, but these meetings should be shorter and much less dreaded. They should become part of the ongoing fabric of the relationship between managers and their subordinates, not an HR mandated add-on.

If effective performance discussions and goal setting become central to the very fabric of the relationship between a manager and his or her talent and an organization's culture, it may be appropriate to eliminate formal performance management meetings entirely. There may not need to be formal review meetings on a predetermined schedule. Instead, managers will "check in" with talent to be sure of what talent development needs to take place, which performance goals are in place, and which goals have been accomplished.

What is done in an effective performance management program is in many ways simply good management. But the reality is that many managers need a support structure to behave as "good" managers. They need support systems to be sure that they set goals, give ongoing feedback, and hold development meetings with the talent that reports to them. In the best of all organizational worlds, they would not need a "system" to get them to do this, but such a world does not exist in most organizations, so performance management systems that are a core piece of an organization's talent management process are needed.

USE TECHNOLOGY

Information technology can help make performance management a more dynamic and effective process. It can make it easy for managers and their talent to communicate on an ongoing basis, and when needed to quickly update and change goals and provide ongoing feedback about goal accomplishment. An increasing number of organizations are utilizing mobile apps to make it easy to have regular communication concerning activities and results. They provide regular check-ins and agile goal management. Yes, this can also be done on the phone or in person, but in many respects it is often easier and better to do via e-mail, a social media platform, or a mobile app. The important point is that technology can help managers track talent behavior and be sure that it is aligned with the organization's strategy and the goals of individuals.

A major advantage of using e-mails, tweets, and other forms of Internet communication is that they can provide an ongoing log of how an individual has performed over a period of time. This can be useful when it comes time to look at development needs, performance, and the distribution of rewards. A common problem in performance evaluations is that since the performance being reviewed typically covers a long period of time (e.g., a year), it is easy to forget the performance that occurred early in the time period. This can mean an unfairly low or high rating for someone who has performed differently over the course of the performance period. Consulting an ongoing communication and work record can help prevent this from happening.

MEASURE EFFECTIVENESS

It is critical that the effectiveness of performance management appraisals be measured. This is the only way to hold managers accountable for how they execute this process and to improve it. Without measurement, managers cannot be held accountable for how effectively they are executing the performance management processes with their talent, and accountability is critical to making performance management a high priority activity that is done well. All too often how well performance management is done is not measured, and as a result it becomes a low priority when it comes to how managers spend their time and how much management development takes place to help them do appraisals well.

One way to measure the effectiveness of an organization's performance management system is to do regular surveys of how the fairness and effectiveness of the system is judged by the organization's talent.

Evaluation data can also be developed based on "pulse" surveys and so-cial media chat about them. It is important to get data on all the key parts: goal setting, feedback, evaluation, and reward allocation.

It is important to reward managers for how effectively they do per-formance management. One interesting approach is to reward them by making their work area a performance-appraisal-free zone. As already mentioned, if managers are effective, formal performance appraisals may not need to be done at all because setting goals and feedback are "just" good management.

In some respects, performance management systems are nothing more than a way to motivate managers and guide their behavior to get them to do something they should be doing anyway. That said, the real-ity is that many managers need a formal system to improve their effec-tiveness at guiding and motivating their employees. Thus, it makes sense to have formal performance appraisal methods that employ the paper-work, scales, and other technology that are part of an effective perfor-mance management system.

The option of having a performance-appraisal-free zone, of course, only makes sense if in fact the individuals in that area do not need appraisals because they are aware of what their goals are and are moti-vated to achieve them. Further, the goals need to be in line with the business strategy and individuals need to receive good feedback about their performance from the work itself or from their managers.

At this point there are no organizations that I am aware in which the idea of performance-appraisal-free zones has been put into place, but it is an interesting idea and one that may eventually gain traction. It cer-tainly makes a lot more sense than organizations simply eliminating performance management for all their employees because they are not executing it effectively.

THERE SHOULD BE NO RATINGS

In traditional appraisal systems, the performance of individuals is judged and a score or set of scores given to each individual. In many systems, individuals are rated or ranked on multiple traits (e.g., dependability, effort, honesty, etc.). The score can come in many different forms. It may be a simple 1–3 rating or it may be a more greatly differentiated rating.

In some organizations, it is a serial ranking. Individuals in specific work areas, or in some cases the whole organization, are ranked against each other from 1 to infinity. Not surprisingly, research has shown that ratings and rankings are subject to all kinds of rater error: some raters are too liberal, some are too rigorous, some have trouble separating performers, some have racial and gender biases, and so on.

One of the worst practices that organizations use is the forced distribution ratings approach, which requires managers to rate the individuals who work for them based on an arbitrary preset distribution of how many outstanding performers, middle performers, and so on they have working for them. Often the percentages are set to fit a statistical normal curve—that is, one where there are an equal number of good and bad performers and a large number of middle performers. The assumption here is that performance in organizations is normally distributed.

It is true that normal distributions do exist, but they only occur with random events. Presumably, behavior in organizations, and particularly performance related behavior, is not a random event in most organizations. Instead it is an event that is carefully prescribed, trained for, and rewarded. Thus, in most effective organizations good performance is a common type of behavior and poor performance is rare. Further, even if the individual levels of performance in an organization are random, it takes a large number of cases—often thousands—for any outcome to produce a normal distribution. Thus, forcing an individual manager to fit his or her ratings of a few direct reports to a predetermined normal curve is almost always going to require wrong placements and produce indefensible results. All too often this leads to appraisers defending the ratings they give by saying "they made me do it." This can damage the entire credibility of the appraisal process and lead to a negative reaction on the part of both the appraiser and appraisee.

The only thing worse than the forced distribution process is the forced ranking approach, which requires appraisers to rank individuals in order from 1 to infinity. For years ExxonMobil ranked its population of engineers from 1 through 6,000+. This approach asks appraisers to make many discriminations that are impossible to make. It is usually very hard to make a valid distinction between somebody who is the tenth best performer and somebody who is the eleventh best. It is usually impossible to determine who ranks 1,102th and who ranks 1,103th. As a result, many of the distinctions that are made are random and indefensible.

In many appraisal systems, individuals are rated or ranked on multiple personal traits (e.g., dependability, effort, honesty, etc.). Ratings that are based on traits are particularly likely to be defective as they are subject to multiple interpretations of what they mean and to biases. Moreover, in many cases they are not behaviors that can be observed, nor are they the most important behaviors for a particular role. As a result, such ratings often lead to charges of discrimination, and the net effect is to damage the credibility of the entire talent management process of an organization.

The alternative to systems that rate and rank individuals is obvious: having performance discussions and feedback about goal accomplishment, but no scoring of individuals. In recent years ratingless performance reviews have become increasingly popular; Adobe and Cambia Health Solutions are among the organizations that use them. Not surprisingly, they are considered a preferable option by many individuals because there is no labeling of individuals based on a score that often seems arbitrary and capricious—not to mention indefensible.

Some organizations use phantom or secret ratings, which are ratings that are made by managers but are never revealed to those who are rated. This has a positive side in that it eliminates the anxiety and often negative reaction that is common when individuals find out what their rating is. Further, it provides a basis for distributing performance-based rewards (e.g. pay). But it does not necessarily improve the validity of the score that is given, and it also may obscure the relationship between pay and performance.

Overall, a convincing case can be made for having ratingless appraisals if managers are willing and able to give good descriptive performance feedback. The major question when no scores are given is: How do decisions about individuals' pay raises, bonuses, promotions, and development needs and opportunities get made without them? They clearly still need to be made and meaningfully described to individuals. Fortunately, there are processes that can be used.

One alternative approach to managers giving ratings is to go directly to decisions about development and pay increases. There is no "intermediate" scoring. One way to make these decisions is to use calibration meetings and to combine them with good feedback to individuals about achievement, success, skill levels, and competencies. The calibration method is used by a number of companies (an early user was General Electric). It brings together groups of managers who have oversight of and insights into performance of multiple individuals and has them discuss the performance and development needs of those individuals and assign pay changes and development opportunities. The results are then communicated to the individuals through their managers.

The calibration group process is complex and can often be time consuming, but it can be effective when multiple managers have good data on the performance of the individuals being appraised and the skills needed to give good feedback. It is an effective method for eliminating the leniency and stringency biases of individual managers and motivating them to develop good performance measures. The managers are required to defend their decisions when it comes to things like pay increases, and as a result they need to have data and are less likely to give ratings that are too favorable or unfavorable and poorly developed.

Typically, calibration meetings happen annually. This puts the responsibility on individual managers to accumulate performance data over the year, bring it to the meeting, and present it effectively to other managers. Calibration meetings usually are held throughout an organization and at all levels. Everyone is appraised based on multiple observers of their performance, and a high level of awareness of the performance of individuals and their career direction is developed in the organization. It also increases the organization's focus on talent and provides useful input for its business strategy. When using calibration meetings it is important to be sure the group making decisions uses good processes; without good processes there is a very real danger of the group making poor decisions because a few members dominate or limited information is presented.

SOCIAL MEDIA AND CROWDSOURCING

Social media can provide important information with respect to the performance of talent. This is, of course, particularly true of the behavior of talent that is not seen by the appraisers themselves. In many cases, managers do not see the behavior of remote sales individuals or even the interaction of individuals in supervisor-subordinate, peer group, and customer situations. This raises the question of whether data should be gathered from those individuals who have a significant chance to observe the critical behavior of talent even though they are not in managerial or supervisory positions with respect to the individuals. Historically it has not been that easy to access such data, and thus it is not typically done.

With social media, crowdsourcing, and the type of customer service information that is now available to organizations, it is technically and practically possible to gather data that shed light on performance. There is little doubt that such data should be gathered and fed back to the individual; this can be an important form of feedback about how individuals are performing and thus help to guide their behavior.

It is not always advisable that social media and crowdsourcing data from employees' peers and others in and outside the organization be used by managers to evaluate the performance of the talent that works for them. The risks of using such data are many, but perhaps the most important one is that it may be biased and inaccurate for any number of reasons. For example, in the case of data coming from an individual's peers, there may be competition at play. As a result, an individual's peers may give a negative evaluation because they themselves are in line for the same promotions and pay raises.

An extreme example of how closely employees can be monitored with social media is provided by the firm Bridgewater Associates. At Bridgewater, employees constantly rate each other on over sixty attributes. Employees are questioned about the outcome of meetings and it is expected that every meeting where at least three employees are present will be subject to evaluation. This system feeds data into a program that has a growing set of benchmarks comparing employees to each other. Ultimately the results lead to smaller bonuses and even the firing of those employees who are poorly rated by their peers. Employees also can get feedback about how a conversation or meeting is going by using an app to retrieve it in real time.

With respect to social media, perhaps the best way to summarize its use is to say that great caution is needed. Social media can potentially provide good feedback and a valuable record of an individual's performance, but it also can potentially be biased as a result of the position

and characteristics of the individuals who are contributing the feedback; an evaluation of this must be taken into account when the data
are considered. This is a prime case in which data analysis should be
used to detect rating biases and other problems.

THE PROCESS SHOULD BE BASED ON DATA

It is increasingly possible to base performance appraisals on objective behavior and activity data rather than opinion. It has always been clear that
the more actual performance data can be brought to the performance
management system, the more effective that system is likely to be. The
problem has been that for many jobs and situations there is no good data
to cover many of the types of behaviors that should be appraised. As a
result, the appraisals end up being made on a mix of subjective opinions,
observations, hard data, activity patterns, and perceptions.

It is clear that in the future there will be an increasing amount of behavioral activity data available to help organizations judge and monitor
the performance of employees. For example, wearable technology is rapidly developing that can track an individual's location and work efforts.
Given this development, it is critical that there be understanding of
which data will go to the talent, which data will go to the organization,
and how the information will be used.

Appraisals based on behavioral data are particularly likely to be used
in warehouse, delivery, and other work where individuals are constantly
moving around to do their work. They can also be used in situations
where individuals are operating company equipment off-site. Data can
also be gathered from individuals who are at workstations or on computers most of the day. In many cases it is easy to monitor their daily
production as well as their hours and minutes of work. When ongoing performance data can be (and is) collected, it is critical that there be
an understanding about what kind of performance data and what kind
of standards will come into play when performance appraisals and
judgments are based on them.

One business where technology and data have transformed talent
management is sports. For example, in baseball data are now available on
the speed and location of every pitch and hit. This allows managers and
executives to go beyond batting averages and earned run averages when

they make development, recruiting, and playing decisions. They can get instant data about pitch speed, arm angle, and force on the elbow and can make immediate decisions about replacing a pitcher, or they can tell whether a batter is hitting the ball well. In basketball, an incredible amount of performance data is now available that shows how individuals and the teams they are on perform in almost every situation.

In many respects the development of big data job behavior has the possibility of transforming the performance review. It can go from an opinion-based discussion between supervisors and subordinates to a data-driven discussion of how an individual is performing based on measures and goals that both the talent and manager see as relevant and are able to continually monitor. This is just the kind of situation that should lead to improved performance and a better understanding of the performance of individuals, groups, and organizations. It can also transform performance management from a dreaded annual meeting between superiors and subordinates to an ongoing feedback discussion and problem-solving activity. Difficult decisions will still have to be made about pay, promotions, terminations, and training, but new technology does create the possibility that there will be a better understanding of why and how such decisions are made.

One final point is that it is particularly important that data be collected and analyzed in real time when organizations are appraising gig workers and other short-term employees. In these cases, the workers often only have a brief relationship with the organization and thus it is important to monitor as closely as possible how individuals are performing in real time. Collecting data on an ongoing basis can give managers the opportunity to intervene and fix problems that otherwise might go unattended and uncorrected until individuals have finished their gig. In particular, if individuals are candidates for additional work after a short gig, it is vital that data be readily available about how they performed on their first gig with the organization.

THE APPRAISAL PROCESS

The growth of distance working and social media raises interesting questions with respect to the comfort and effectiveness of individuals conducting appraisals via e-mail, video, apps, and social networks. Do performance management discussions need to be face-to-face? For a long time it has been assumed that nothing can or should substitute for an in-person discussion between the appraiser and the appraisee. That was probably a good rule years ago, when individuals were not so used to communicating via e-mail and the social media, but today it seems obsolete and inefficient.

Yes, people may take more risks if they are communicating via technology such as e-mail, but they are also much more accustomed to communicating this way than they used to be and may be more clear, articulate, direct, thoughtful, and comfortable communicating via social media and technology. Perhaps the best way to determine whether a performance review should take place in a face-to-face meeting, using visual tools, or by e-mail is to look at how the individuals normally interface in their work situation. If they do often communicate via e-mail or other forms of technology, then perhaps that is also the best way to conduct the performance review. On the other hand, if they are colocated and on a regular basis talk to each other, it probably does not make sense to go to social media or e-mail to do the performance review. Perhaps it could start that way but conclude in person.

CONCLUSION

The key relationships between performance management and the new strategic talent management are shown in table 7.1. It shows that performance management needs to change significantly to be in alignment with realities in the new workforce, workplace, and environment.

Having an effective performance management system is a key to implementing the strategy of an organization. When a system operates effectively, it can turn a strategy into organizational behavior. But it can only do so if it is driven and supported by managers who can turn the business strategy into goals and objectives for the behavior of individuals and the key units of an organization.

Skills and performance are at the core of what a performance management system should be about. It should motivate the right types of skill development and be based on valid, meaningful, and timely assessments of performance. As has been noted in this chapter, this is increasingly possible today with the better measures that exist and the

Table 7.1 Performance management

Strategy driven	Goals and measures used are driven by the strategy
Skills based	Assess skills and set development goals
Performance focused	Use measureable performance goals
Agile	Use frequent goal setting and performance reviews to adjust for strategic change
Segmented	Adapt process to type of work measures and skills of participants
Evidence based	Appraise the appraisers and measure the outcomes of the process

type and amount of data that can be collected in an increasing number of today's workplaces.

The diversity of today's organizations and their talent calls strongly for a variety of different practices in the area of performance management. No performance management system or approach is likely to be the best one for all or even many organizations—or, for that matter, for all parts of any organization that exists today. Based on the nature of the organization, the work, and the talent, successful performance management systems may very well need to use different types of measures, different frequencies, and different relationships to reward systems. They also may require different behaviors on the part of managers.

The key to decisions with respect to what the right behaviors are to measure and what segments to create should primarily be driven by what is measureable and how frequently and in what way the key organizational outcomes can be measured. To some degree this will be determined by the activity that is being examined and by the hierarchical level that is the focus of performance management activities. Also important are the skills of managers and the kind of technology that can be utilized.

Performance management judgments and evaluations need to become much more data- and evidence-based. Data also need to be gathered on how effective an organization's appraisal systems are, on what is working and what is not working, and on how well individuals are actually carrying out the appraisal process. The performance management process is too important a process to be left to chance; it needs to be based on evidence of effectiveness and supported by an ongoing measurement system that focuses on how it is being implemented and is impacting performance.

Overall, performance management is an area that requires major changes to be effective in the workplace of the future. It has not been effective in the past, and it is only going to be less effective if the same practices that have been used for decades continue to be used. A thoughtful data-based performance management system is badly needed in most organizations. Given the technology and knowledge that is currently available, it is possible that effective performance management systems can be designed and utilized by organizations. Because of the nature of the current workplace and workforce, performance management has never been more important than it is today, and it has never been so possible to do it effectively.

8

ORGANIZING FOR TALENT MANAGEMENT

The talent management systems and practices that fit the new world of work, workers, and organizations require compatible organization designs. They cannot be managed and used by organizations and human resources (HR) functions that are designed to operate with traditional talent management systems, and many of them are not likely to be effective in traditional hierarchical organizations.

The key issue here is system fit. The classic "star" model of organization design that is shown in figure 8.1 makes this point. It shows that for an organization to operate effectively, its five key systems must fit each other. The implications of this for organization design and talent management are clear. Both the talent management practices of an organization and how the HR function is organized and managed need to be changed to fit the new world of organizations, with their new management processes, talent, organization structures, and work processes. System fit is the key to successfully reinventing talent management for the new world of work.

HR functions that are not strategically oriented, value standardization over individualization, and are not based on modern information technology simply cannot design, implement, and operate talent management principles and practices that fit the new world of work. To implement and operate many of the principles and practices that have

Figure 8.1

been discussed thus far, a very different kind of organization structure is needed for the HR function as well as the total organization: one that is agile, can offer multiple systems and segmentation, is strategically driven, and in which talent is one of the most important contributors to its operation and effectiveness. In such a structure, talent needs to be managed strategically from top to bottom. It needs to include technology that until recently has not been used by HR functions and needs to be driven by agile business strategies and organization designs that enable talented individuals to do complex knowledge work.

HR functions are required that differ from those of traditional bureaucratic organizations in how they are structured, staffed, and operated. Important changes in how the top management and boards of organizations operate and are staffed are also needed. Organizations need to be able to make talent management decisions that fit their overall structure and strategy and that are based on data and talent management expertise.

THE CORPORATE BOARD

Corporate board members, like chief executive officers (CEOs), often say that talent is an organization's most important asset, but in most cases their boards are not structured, operated, and staffed with this as a guiding principle. Quite to the contrary, they do not know what constitutes good talent management and practice and what that looks like in the type of complex organizations they govern. They also do not get the information about their organizations' talent management operations and effectiveness that they need to make good talent management decisions.

The problems with boards start with their membership: they typically have at most one member who has in-depth expertise in talent management, and most boards do not have even one such member. They make the incorrect and all-too-common assumption that they know how to manage people. They often do not ask for or get reports on the condition of the talent in the organization. They also, all too often, do not operate effectively as decision-making teams. The one talent management aspect in which they do spend a considerable amount of time and hire experts for help with is hiring outside senior executives and sometimes for recruiting new board members. They also get outside expertise and help with board and executive compensation matters. But in the talent management areas that involve the organization's operations (e.g., engagement, development, performance management) all too often they do not have or seek expertise.

Boards need help to make informed decisions about what talent management practices should be like throughout their organizations. They also need help in gathering and interpreting data about how effectively the human capital part of their organization is functioning, and in making changes and corrections to the human capital operations of it so that it will be agile and be able to change and provide a competitive advantage.

What is required for boards to have adequate knowledge in the area of talent management? First, each board needs at least one member who is an expert in the field; this is the only way to be sure that there is someone in board meetings who has the necessary power, expertise, and credibility to support an organization having the right human capital management practices.

Boards can and should utilize consultants and draw on the expertise of the internal HR staff for advice. This is a good practice for an organization to adopt, but it is not enough. It is quite unlikely that the best decisions about talent management can be reached by boards on a regular basis without somebody actually on the board who can suggest, validate, and vote for them. There is simply no substitute for having a board member who is a knowledgeable talent management expert.

Second, boards should have a source of expertise in the area of human capital and talent management in the form of a chief human resource officer (CHRO) who regularly attends board meetings. All too often this does not happen even in large corporations. This is just the opposite of what happens with respect to the chief financial officer (CFO), who is almost always present at board meetings alongside many members of the board who are also knowledgeable in finance because they are from the investment community.

In many respects, what boards need to make good talent decisions is similar to what they need to make good financial decisions. The CHRO, like the CFO, needs to be present at most board meetings, and board members are needed who are knowledgeable in talent management. Only with this combination will boards be able to intelligently discuss options and arrive at the right decisions with respect to the talent of an organization and its management systems. This is particularly true with respect to understanding and acting on the kind of talent management effectiveness data that an organization's board should review on a regular basis.

Just as they review quarterly earnings statements and in some cases monthly statements, boards need to regularly review the human capital data for their organization. The information reviewed should include not just traditional absenteeism, turnover, and recruiting data but also data about engagement and satisfaction, as well as a skills-based strategic inventory of the talent their organization has. Finally, there should be information about the agility of the organization.

How often should talent data be reviewed by boards? In most organizations this should happen at minimum on a quarterly basis. With the rate of change that exists both in the business environment and the mobility of talent, a quarterly assessment is likely to be the right option for most organizations. In some more stable traditional organizations, a semiannual assessment may be enough.

All corporate boards have multiple committees that meet regularly to review operations in specific areas; for example, every board has an audit committee and finance committee. Yet few boards have a talent committee. Again, this is a case where organizations and boards say one thing, "talent is our most important asset," but behave differently.

A corporate board should have a talent committee that reviews the condition of the organization's talent on a regular basis and regularly reports to the full board on its condition and the condition of its talent management systems. The talent committee needs to focus on more than just the executive talent in the organization; it needs to look at the condition of all the talent, with a particular focus on key talent. Only by doing this can it inform the board about what should be done when talent is discussed in board meetings.

The challenge that boards face is acting like they talk when it comes to talent. They need to stop just saying talent is our organization's most important asset—and start "walking the walk" when it comes to talent. In many cases this means structuring and behaving with respect to how talent is managed at the board level in a way that is very similar to the way financial assets are handled. The boards need to have expertise, get regular data, review the data, and act when there are problems.

THE EXECUTIVE TEAM

The top executive team of every corporation needs to be involved in the making of key talent decisions. It needs to understand the design of the talent management systems, assure that design is operating effectively, and in the case of key appointments be sure that the right individuals are chosen. To make the executive team function effectively when it makes talent decisions, a high level of talent management expertise is required. Such expertise is rarely present in the CEO.

The CEOs of most organizations have little or no background in talent management. Yes, they have experience in making talent management decisions as a result of their previous management jobs, but rarely have they had a job in HR or talent management or any kind of formal training or education with respect to talent management. The top executive team of an organization needs to include at least one individual who is a talent management expert and who is able to detail and strategically clarify how talent management is related to business strategy and operations.

One obvious candidate for the role of talent expert on the top management team is the CHRO. Yet in about half of U.S. corporations the CHRO does not report to the CEO; instead the reporting relationship is to the chief operating officer (COO). In a significant number of organizations, the CHRO does not have a background in talent management and HR. This may be appropriate in those situations where talent is not a key source of competitive advantage, but in most organizations that is not the case. When the CHRO does not have a background in HR, it may be appropriate to have the chief talent officer (CTO) involved in all top management decisions about talent.

There are several organization design approaches that can be used to be sure that a top executive team has the expertise and input it needs to make effective talent management decisions. The most obvious one has already been mentioned—a CHRO with experience in HR and talent management as a member of the executive team. In situations where in-depth expertise with respect to talent is needed, a CTO can be included as an adviser and contributor to talent decisions. Often even CHROs who have experience in HR do not have in-depth expertise in talent management because their job combines managing both the administrative and strategic sides of HR and, as a result, they may not have time to delve deeply into some talent management issues.

It clearly does not make sense to have the CHRO report to the COO in situations where talent is a key source of competitive advantage for an organization; in these situations reporting should be to the CEO. One option here is to split the HR function into two functions: an administrative one and a strategic performance one. This is much like what happened with finance, where accounting was separated from finance, and also what happened with marketing and sales. With the split, the operational side of HR will report to the COO while the strategic elements of HR and talent management will report to the CEO.

There are multiple ways to structure the top management levels of an organization to ensure that talent gets the proper strategic and operational consideration. The one thing that always needs to happen is that key business strategic decisions consider and are influenced by talent management factors, and that talent management decisions are influenced by key business and strategy decisions and factors. This can only occur if business decision-making forums have a strong talent management perspective. This in turn is only likely to happen if, at a minimum, the CHRO or the CTO plays an active role in business strategy development and in major strategy implementations. It also, of course, requires that the CTO or CHRO has a good knowledge of the business and understands the relationship between talent management practices and policies and the development and implementation of business strategies.

THE CHIEF ORGANIZATIONAL EFFECTIVENESS OFFICER

Some organizations may be best structured by having a chief organizational effectiveness officer (COEO) who is a member of the senior management team and reports directly to the CEO. This position should have reporting to it the traditional HR function, organization design, organization development, business strategy, and talent management. The key to effectiveness here is finding someone to fill the COEO role who can bring together the multiple types of expertise and disciplines that influence an organization's effectiveness. This person needs to understand talent management, and also the operation of an HR function, the basics of organization design, change management, and business strategy.

As organizations become increasingly complex in today's economy, a design that is based on a COEO makes particularly good sense. It puts someone clearly in charge of the management systems of an organization. The COEO can participate in business decision making at the top level and can provide expertise about the capabilities of the organization and what it takes to make that organization operate effectively, including conversations about business strategy and competitive advantage.

One organization that has implemented a COEO type organization structure is Jack in the Box. This fast food restaurant business has a top management position that it calls chief people, culture, and corporate strategy officer. This executive vice president position reports to the CEO and attends all board meetings.

THE CHIEF TALENT OFFICER

As already suggested, most organizations need to have a chief talent officer. This position should be the human capital counterpart to the financial capital part of an organization. The latter, of course, is typically called the CFO and reports directly to the CEO. The CFO usually attends board meetings and is a critical member of the top management team. The same kind of role needs to be played by the CTO and/or the CHRO. As already noted, either the CHRO or the CTO needs to regularly attend board meetings and committee meetings to be sure that human capital is given proper consideration when strategic decisions are made.

At this point there is no single, universally right answer to the question of whom the CTO should report to. It depends in part upon the degree of criticality that human capital has to an organization and, of course, how the job is defined and filled. In an organization in which talent is unquestionably the major asset, the CTO and CHRO should in most cases report to the CEO and be a part of the senior management team. In cases where talent is not as pivotal for the success of the organization, it may make sense to have the CTO report to the CHRO, and have the CHRO be the overall representative of the talent side of the organization.

Interesting organization design possibilities exist when organizations have both a CEO and a COO. In this case, it is possible to create a split reporting relationship for the roles of the CHRO and CTO. One option is to have the CTO report to the CEO while having the CHRO report to the COO. With this design, much of the strategic talent management and HR work would be controlled by the CEO with input from the CTO, while the operations side of HR would be controlled by the CHRO and the COO. The advantage here is that the human capital management strategy of the organization and the systems that support it can be created and managed in a strategic manner. Frequently they are criti-cized, and often correctly so, for being too operational and failing to take a business strategy–driven approach to human capital management. Having the CTO report to the CEO is particularly likely to be appropri-ate when the CHRO reports to the COO. In this case the CHRO may not have the key strategic involvement that is necessary to make critical decisions about how the talent management system should be managed and talent positioned.

Overall, it is clear that there is not one right organization design for talent management that fits all talent critical organizations. It is clear that they need a strong focus on talent, and having a CTO is a positive way to make this happen. How the CTO position fits into the larger organization depends on the type of business, its strategy, and the kind of competitive advantage that the organization seeks. This may be quite different, for example, in a talent-intensive business than it would be in one that is driven by financial capital. In all cases, however, simply hav-ing an HR function with the usual administrative departments of com-pensation and benefits, training, and selection and placement is no longer the right way to go. Organizations need to be designed with tal-ent management structures that determine and are determined by an organization strategy and that integrate and prioritize the effective management of talent.

WORKFORCE ANALYTICS

Organizations need to have a talent analytics function. Admittedly it cannot be very large in smaller organizations because of the associated cost. But smaller organizations can get valuable help from consultants, gig talent, and professional associations. In major corporations, how-ever, talent analytics can and should be a well-funded and well-staffed group that reports to the CTO (or in the absence of a CTO, the CHRO) and focuses on gathering, analyzing, and translating data into action. A talent analytics group should be staffed by individuals who can gather, analyze, and convert data into evidence-based talent management decisions and actions.

Gathering and analyzing data is, of course, just the first step in hav-ing a successful talent analytics process; data have to be correctly interpreted, and practices and operational changes that are based on them must be implemented. This requires keeping those who have to manage and implement change informed on a continuous basis about what data are being gathered and how they should be interpreted, and then getting them involved in developing and implementing the solutions that are suggested by those data. This, of course, means that an organization has to have an effective organization development function that is paired with the talent analytics function. Left by themselves, groups that simply analyze talent data can be out of touch with the reality of an organization, and although they do good research, they do research that is not implementable or implemented. One key to gathering data that is useful is to have the users participate in determining which data are collected.

For decades, AT&T, General Electric, IBM, and other large organizations have had analytics groups that gather and analyze data on talent behavior and costs. Google has a major talent analytics group that has had a significant impact on its talent management strategy. One area where it has been particularly active and effective is attrition. Google has developed models that predict and practices that help prevent turnover.

The major challenge that talent-driven organizations face is managing their talent in a way that reflects the growing complexity of the world of work. Analytic data can help with this, but only if they are collected on the right issues and in a way that leads to the individuals who have to implement talent management systems understanding them, being motivated to utilize them, and being able to implement what they suggest. Creating this kind of situation requires an organization that is talent driven, talent sensitive, and organized to effectively manage talent.

CONCLUSION

The design of an organization is critical to its being able to properly manage its talent. Because of the changes in the nature of talent management, HR needs to be structured in a way that allows it to be strategy driven. As is shown in table 8.1, this requires the corporate board to have a knowledgeable talent management member. The presence of the CHRO, COEO, or CTO of the organization at board meetings can be a key resource for boards. Their presence can facilitate the development

Table 8.1 Organization design

Strategy driven	CHRO board presence; board members with talent expertise
Skills based	CTO senior management position
Performance focused	Talent decisions and practices influenced by management approach
Agile	Talent decisions integrated with strategy and organization design changes
Segmented	Analytics that can show differences in results and preferences by segments
Evidence based	Analytics group that creates talent management evidence

of a business strategy that is aligned with what happens in the talent management area and can help design talent management practices and operate systems that effectively implement that strategy. In many cases this means bringing a skills-based orientation to the design of talent management systems. Simply stated, strategy needs to drive the competencies an organization has because the right skills are needed in order to execute an organization's strategy.

To be performance based, the organization design of talent management activities needs to be driven by the type of performance that is required by the organization. It needs to influence the analytics activities of the talent management part of the organization, and talent management needs to be measured on the basis of its impact on the overall performance of the organization.

As is shown in table 8.1, agility comes into play when the strategy changes and talent management practices need to change and be adapted. This is the reason behind putting the CTO into the strategy discussion and for having him or her report to senior management. The strategy of the organization should also be partially determined by and determine the type of segmentation that exists in the organization's HR systems. Understanding the type of segmentation that is needed should be facilitated by having talent management executives involved in discussions and decisions about business strategy and operations.

Overall, a new design of the HR function is clearly needed for talent management to operate effectively. The traditional organization design of the HR function was never intended to have talent operate as a strategic driver of the business nor to respond to a rapidly changing world of work, workers, and organizations. Merely giving HR a "seat at the table" is not the answer; it must be a major force in developing and implementing talent management principles and practices that are major drivers of organizational effectiveness.

9

TALENT MANAGEMENT REINVENTED

C reating an effective strategic talent management system that fits the new world of work, workers, and organizations is not just a matter of adopting a few of the different talent management principles and practices that have been discussed in the earlier chapters of this book; it requires adopting an integrated set of policies and practices that fit with an organization's strategy and its environment. This point was made in chapter 2 and is basic to figure 2.1, which shows a need for the five major talent management systems in an organization to be integrated with each other. Previous chapters have outlined the practices and policies that need to be adopted by organizations in each of these five areas. Adopting them is fundamental in creating organizations that have strategic talent management systems.

For talent management to be a strategic advantage for an organization, integrated systems are required. Simply changing pay practices and selection practices is not sufficient to produce the kind of organizational performance that will provide competitive advantage for an organization. Indeed, just adopting a few changes in an area or change in just a few areas runs the risk of making any organization much less effective than it would be if it used an integrated set of traditional performance management packages. When it comes to talent management, reinvention is a systemic issue and not a single policy or small set of changes in practice. It requires an aligned and congruent set of policy and practice changes that involve all five major areas of talent management.

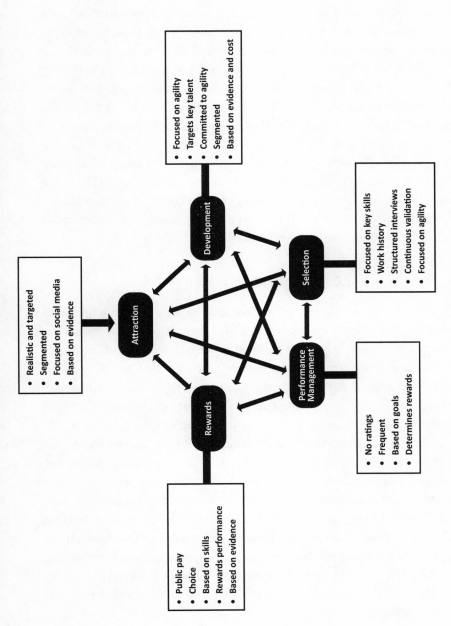

Figure 9.1

- Realistic and targeted
- Segmented
- Focused on social media
- Based on evidence

Attraction

- Focused on agility
- Targets key talent
- Committed to agility
- Segmented
- Based on evidence and cost

Development

- Focused on key skills
- Work history
- Structured interviews
- Continuous validation
- Focused on agility

Selection

- Public pay
- Choice
- Based on skills
- Rewards performance
- Based on evidence

Rewards

- No ratings
- Frequent
- Based on goals
- Determines rewards

Performance Management

Figure 9.1 shows the key practices that need to be utilized in each of the five talent management areas. Some organizations may practice a few of them, but that is not a sufficient reinvention of their talent management systems for them to become strategically effective. Indeed, it is unlikely to do much to increase—and may even decrease—the performance of an organization. Overall, the effectiveness of an organization is only likely to be significantly improved if most, if not all, of the principles and practices are adopted. The reason for this is simple: they reinforce each other in ways that make them mutually effective. It takes a combination of them to produce the kind of behavior and performance that organizations need in today's highly competitive, rapidly changing business environment. Together they create a strategic talent management approach that is strategy driven, skills based, performance focused, agile, segmented, and evidence based.

TALENT MANAGEMENT CHANGE

Creating talent management systems that include the principles and practices described in this book and fit the new world of work is relatively easy in agile, high-involvement organizations that value people and believe in information and power sharing. They "fit!" Instead of massive change in how these organizations manage talent, what they need is systematic learning, testing, and further development. Many of them already practice some or many of the talent management strategies and practices described in earlier chapters. But what about traditional bureaucratic organizations? Should they and can they change their talent management approach?

One thing traditional organizations can and should do, if they have not already done so, is to adopt those universal best practices that can help improve performance in both traditional and agile, high-involvement organizations. These practices range from improving their performance management systems to being sure that they have valid data-based attraction and selection systems as well as reward systems that motivate performance.

Changes in information technology and systems now make it possible for most organizations, even traditionally managed ones, to greatly improve their talent management practices and systems. They can make them faster, more responsive, more segmented, and more user-friendly. But unless traditional organizations change the way they are organized and managed, they will not gain all the benefits that are possible from changing their talent management practices—and indeed, adopting some of the practices may make them more dysfunctional. The primary reason for this is that the practices are designed to make talent a key source of organizational effectiveness, and this is not possible in a traditional bureaucratic organization. As a result, some of the changes in talent management suggested in this book may make them less effective. For example, making pay rates public may lead to mistrust, while segmentation may lead to unmanageable administrative complexity; both could lead to employee dissatisfaction. Paying for skills and involving peers in performance reviews and selection decisions may have a negative impact on performance and talent engagement.

Overall, many traditional bureaucratic organizations can (and most should) change how they manage talent, but this should not be a stand-alone change. It needs to be part of an integrated change effort that is targeted at changing all the points on the star model (see figure 8.1); changing only one or two points on the star is likely to make the organization less effective. Similarly, changing one or a few talent management practices is not likely to have a significant positive impact on organizational effectiveness.

The reality is that large-scale change in how they are managed is needed for traditional organizations to effectively reinvent their talent management practices. Perhaps the most important implication of this is that a talent management change process that is directed toward creating strategic talent management processes and practices cannot be led by the chief human resource officer (CHRO) and the human resources (HR) function. It needs to be led by the CEO and the top management team. The reason for this is clear: change needs to be organization wide and affect multiple systems. There definitely is a critical role for HR to play: it is to be the expert resource and to be willing and eager to change its talent management systems when the time is right. What it cannot and should not try to do in a traditionally managed and structured organization is lead a talent management system change effort that is not part of a larger organizational change effort that is supported by senior management.

One final point concerning strategic talent management change is worth repeating. In most organizational change efforts, talent management change should not be a stand-alone change. It is best positioned as part of an overall change effort that covers all five points of the star. It should not be the lead change; it is best positioned as a change that is part of an overall effort to create an agile, high-performance, strategy-driven organization. It also can be effective in situations where it is a catch-up change that reinvents talent management so that it fits an already operating high-involvement organization.

CONCLUSION

The time has come for organizations to manage talent in ways that are innovative and maximize the contributions that individuals can make to organizations. Talent is an increasingly important asset of organizations; it needs to be managed in ways that increase its value and utilize it effectively. This can only be done by taking a more strategic approach to talent management and abandoning many of the traditional approaches that have been best practice standard operating procedures for decades. There is no single change in practice that will make talent management a key strategic contributor to organizational effectiveness. It can only happen if organizations adopt an integrated, strategically driven set of principles and practices that recognize people as an important asset and maximize their contribution to organizational effectiveness. What is needed to do this is a comprehensive set of talent management principles and practices that are strategy driven and drive an organization's strategy.

ACKNOWLEDGMENTS

I have been very fortunate to have worked with many great management thinkers who have impacted my thinking about talent management and organizations. I would like to single out the major ones here. During my graduate school years, I was fortunate to have Lyman Porter as my mentor, supervisor, and friend. This relationship continued for over fifty years, and it greatly influenced my work and thinking about motivation and satisfaction.

My first "job" was at Yale University, where I met Chris Argyris, who had a great influence on my thinking about organizational effectiveness and what makes organizational research useful.

My first senior faculty job was at the University of Michigan. I spent my time there at the Institute for Social Research, where I headed one of its research programs. It was a great learning experience, as I had the chance to work with Robert Kahn and Stanley Seashore and learned about field research and organizational change.

At the University of Southern California, I have had the chance to work with an icon in the field of leadership development and organization, Warren Bennis. I also have had the good fortune to work with some of the best talent management thinkers in the corporate and academic worlds as a result of my role in the Center for Effective Organizations; my relationships with all of them helped me develop many of the ideas that are in this book. While at USC, I have done hundreds of studies on talent management. The results of these studies led to the key principles and practices that are the foundation of the reinvented approach to talent management that I advocate in this book.

INDEX

agility principle, 120; organizational branding issue of, 34, 43, 43t; in organizational design, 116, 116t; in performance management, 104t; in reward systems, 88t; selection process analysis of, 58, 58t; in talent, 12; in talent development, 72t 73; in talent management, 23–25, 30, 30t, 43

Amazon, 35

appraisal: gig and short-term worker, 102; performance-free zones in, 96; ratingless, 98; scheduled performance process in, 93; traditional performance, 90

AT&T, 34, 60, 67, 115

Berrett-Koehler, 36

best practice, 1, 20, 29, 57, 60, 67, 120

blind audition, 49

bonus, 78, 81–83

Bridgewater Associates, 100

bureaucratic organization, 1–2, 10–11, 121

chief executive officer (CEO), 10, 110–114, 121; favorite adage of, 15, 108; interview questions of, 52

chief financial officer (CFO), 109, 113

chief human resource officer (CHRO), 109, 111–115, 116t, 121

chief operating officer (COO), 111, 113–114

chief organizational effectiveness officer (COEO), 112–113, 115

chief talent officer (CTO), 111–116, 116t

competitive advantage, 68; of organizations, 26, 36, 66, 108, 111–112, 114, 118; of talent, 11–12, 77; talent management systems as, 15, 23

CrossKnowledge, 65

data: -based decision making in organizations, 29–30; in organizational design, 109–110, 114–115; in performance management, 95, 100–102, 104–105; in selection process, 47–48, 50; in talent management, 28–30

Deutsche Bank, 48

digital assistant, 6

Ernst and Young, 48

evidence based principle, 3, 114, 120; organizational branding as, 43, 43t; organizational decision making as, 29–30; organizational design as, 116t; performance management data and evaluations as, 104–105, 104t; reward systems effectiveness decisions as, 84–85,

88t, 89; selection process, 58t; talent development as, 72t; talent management as, 27–31, 30t, 43–44

ExxonMobil, 34, 97

Facebook, 40, 54

face-to-face versus e-mail review, 102–103

FedEx, 3–4

forced distribution ratings approach, 97

forced ranking approach, 97–98

General Electric, 24, 34, 60, 67, 115

gig or short-term worker, 50, 67–68, 72–73, 78, 114; employer relationship of, 33, 41, 43t; 58, 62; performance pay for, 82–83; and short-term worker appraisals, 102; as talent access approach, 19

Glassdoor, 40, 71, 86

global business environment, 3, 12–13; continuous improvement need in, 5; financial capital availability in, 4; global sourcing in, 4; information technology in, 4; talent as global resource in, 4–5

Google, 4, 9, 29, 35–36, 77, 115

historic organization, 34–35

human resources (HR), 27, 40, 60, 63, 76, 121; administrative and strategic performance split in, 111; functions of, 1–3; in organizational design, 106–107, 112–117; percentage of time spent on roles of, 2t; performance management function of, 91–92

IBM, 24, 29, 34, 60, 67, 115

information technology industry, 3; change creation in, 5–6; digital assistants in, 6; employment relationships in, 6; in global business environment, 4; organization and talent management changes in, 120–121; for performance management, 94–95; workforce development in, 6

interview, 51–53

Jack in the Box, 113

"knowledge worker," 6–7

LinkedIn, 40, 70

Lynda.com, 65

McDonald's, 3

"merit" salary increase, 81

Microsoft, 4, 48

mobile app use, 48, 95

Monster, 40

Myers-Briggs Type Indicator, 51

ABOUT THE AUTHOR

Ed Lawler has devoted his career to studying the relationship between talent and organizations. He began his work as a graduate student at the University of California–Berkeley with research on motivation and satisfaction. Today, he is Distinguished Professor of Business at the University of Southern California's Marshall School of Business. He joined USC in 1978, and in 1979 founded and became director of the University's Center for Effective Organizations, which has been recognized by  *Fortune* and other publications as one of the world's leading management research organizations.

Ed has been honored as a major contributor to theory, research, and practice in the fields of human resources management, compensation, organizational development, and organizational effectiveness. *Business-Week* has proclaimed him one of the top six gurus in the field of management, and *Human Resource Executive* has called him one of the human resource field's most influential people. *Workforce* magazine has identified him as one of the twenty-five visionaries who have shaped today's workplace over the past century. He is the recipient of many awards, including the Society for Human Resource Management's Michael R. Losey Award, of which he was the first recipient. He is also a consultant to many governments and corporations, including the majority of the Fortune 100 companies.

National television appearances include CNBC, CNN, MSNBC, and NBC's *Today*. He is also a frequent speaker to executive and managerial audiences around the globe.

Ed is the author of over four hundred articles and 50 books. His previous book on talent management, *Talent: Making People Your Competitive Advantage* (2008), was a best seller. *Reinventing Talent Management* does not just update that book but redefines what talent management best practices look like. It is based on his many global studies of talent management policies and practices and his research on how organizations, people, and technology are changing.

You can visit Ed Lawler's website at http://www.edwardlawler.com/ and the Center for Effective Organizations' website at https://ceo.usc.edu/.

Berrett–Koehler
Publishers

Connecting people and ideas
to create a world that works for all

Dear Reader,

Thank you for picking up this book and joining our worldwide community of Berrett-Koehler readers. We share ideas that bring positive change into people's lives, organizations, and society.

To welcome you, we'd like to offer you a free e-book. You can pick from among twelve of our bestselling books by entering the promotional code **BKP92E** here: http://www.bkconnection.com/welcome.

When you claim your free e-book, we'll also send you a copy of our e-news-letter, the *BK Communiqué*. Although you're free to unsubscribe, there are many benefits to sticking around. In every issue of our newsletter you'll find

- A free e-book
- Tips from famous authors
- Discounts on spotlight titles
- Hilarious insider publishing news
- A chance to win a prize for answering a riddle

Best of all, our readers tell us, "Your newsletter is the only one I actually read." So claim your gift today, and please stay in touch!

Sincerely,

Charlotte Ashlock
Steward of the BK Website

Questions? Comments? Contact me at bkcommunity@bkpub.com.

Certified
B Corporation
bcorporation.net